Lou Gehrig

THE IRON HORSE OF BASEBALL

THE DURABLE DUTCHMAN

Lou Gehrig

THE IRON HORSE OF BASEBALL

By

RICHARD G. HUBLER

HOUGHTON MIFFLIN COMPANY · BOSTON

The Riverside Press Cambridge

The Riverside Press
CAMBRIDGE · MASSACHUSETTS
PRINTED IN THE U.S.A.

CONTENTS

THE first time I ever saw Lou Gehrig in action was
not in baseball but in football. There was a game
played by Columbia against Dick Harlow's very
powerful Colgate team, which, at that time, was one
of the best in the country. I was very much impressed
by a young Columbia back named Gehrig who, with
the finest possible spirit, continued to play after a
bad arm or shoulder injury.

After that date my admiration for Lou grew steadily. No matter what the situation might be, he had a
quality of character that certainly no one I ever
knew has topped. It was a mixture of strength and
gentleness, of courage and complete cleanness in
everything he did.

For example, there was the occasion of a hunting
trip in Arkansas with Bill Dickey where Lou went
along with the bunch, but admitted that he could
never bring himself to kill anything except a rival
pitcher's fast ball or a curve.

There were times when he would go out with Babe
Ruth and myself at golf, but Lou was always afraid

that the golf swing might interfere with his baseball swing, so he would say, 'Yes, I know this is a great game, but I am going to wait to take it up until I have finished my baseball career.' So he never got his chance at golf.

I think one of the gamest things I ever saw Lou do came after his illness had begun to develop. This was on a fishing trip for white marlin with Bill Dickey and Bucky Harris off Wilmington. I roomed with Lou the night before, and it was pitiful to see the desperate effort he made to take care of himself without bothering anyone else. The next day he caught his fish and brought it in, although I found out later that he was barely able to lift a coffee-pot at the time.

Lou had one of the rarest of all traits, which was an amazing unselfishness and thoughtfulness for the pleasures of others. As far as I knew him I don't believe he ever gave a thought to himself. He had a certain sweetness that is beyond description — something you had to know in personal contact to feel and understand.

And yet with all this he was one of the most determined men and one of the hardest fighters on the field that baseball has ever known. It was again a rare mixture of strength and gentleness. I can't think of anyone to whom the word 'gentleman' would be more applicable than to Lou Gehrig. I mean it in its deeper, fuller meaning.

It is impossible to estimate the tremendous good he did for the youth of this country by the example he set in both his public and his private life. It is something beyond calculation when you consider the millions of younger people interested in sports who followed his career.

As a ballplayer his records of hitting and teamplay will always remain far up on the books. But his best record was not that of home runs or power hitting. It was a durability record — one of honor, fineness, and the highest type of sportsmanship.

GRANTLAND RICE

Little Louie

THE day was June 3, 1932. It was a warm afternoon in Shibe Park, the Philadelphia baseball stadium. A breeze fluttered the flags on the stadium rim; pop and hot-dog vendors, shouting their wares, threaded among the shirt-sleeved fans. The diamond lay green and geometrical below.

The great Yankee team was to play the Philadelphia Athletics.

Hours later the rays of the sun were long, the flags motionless. The vendors were still. The sleek turf of the diamond lay torn by the spiked shoes of the players. The fans, hoarse from shouting, were crowding the exits.

Few of them realized that they had just seen one of baseball's great games. Only in the press box was it known that a star had reached his zenith.

Let the reporters who saw that day tell the story.

Here is the account of the *New York Herald Tribune*:

> Records fell like raindrops in an April shower on this
> sunny June afternoon as Henry Louis Gehrig, the durable
> first-baseman, paved the way for a 20 to 13 victory for the
> Yankees over the Athletics with four home runs in four con-
> secutive times at bat, breaking all modern major league
> marks and tying the two immortals, Robert Lowe and Ed
> Delahanty, who accomplished the feat in the nineties.

Here be it written into the record that Lowe and
Delahanty did their feats in the misty prehistoric ages
of baseball — May 30, 1894, and July 13, 1896, re-
spectively — when records, balls, bats, and players
were open to question. Hammering out a home run
in parks like the Philadelphia Stadium is a gargantuan feat when compared to knocking one over the
fence in one of the early games. Since that day in
1932 only Chuck Klein of the National League Phil-
lies has hit four for four — on July 10, 1936.

> Four times Gehrig came to bat, and four times he pumped
> the ball over the fence or into the distant stands. Twice
> more he stepped to the plate with his mace and from the
> slim crowd of five thousand rose a shrill cry for more home
> runs, but the laddie who is known as Lou had done his
> share.

He had indeed. Only a miracle catch by Al Simmons, one that carried the famous left-fielder, then
playing center field, back, back, back, making him
leap into the air and hang on to the ball by an in-
credible feat of fielding legerdemain — only that kept
Lou from collecting five homers. When Simmons

pulled the ball down, Lou was already well on his way home.

> Lou had carried the Yankees from behind in a thrilling battle that threatened open warfare, with the umpires entering into the hostilities. He had set a pace of pounding for his team-mates to follow and although none could do quite as much, many came close.
>
> Around the nucleus of Gehrig's four home runs the Yankees tied a major league mark when Lazzeri, Combs, and Babe Ruth added one apiece to lift the total for one game by a single club to seven. Around the nucleus of the sixteen bases which those four clouts by Gehrig represented, they broke another modern record with a total of 50 bases for one contest, the former being 46. The Yankees collected 23 hits. Another record was the combined total of 77 bases for the two clubs.

It was seven years and a day from the date that Lou Gehrig had broken into the regular Yankee lineup.

In the clubhouse afterward Lou's team-mates joshed him about losing too many balls for the good of the American League budget. Manager Joe McCarthy, for once showing excitement, came up to greet and congratulate Lou as he came in. The one-and-only Babe Ruth, looming through the fog of shower-steam, pushing through the heavy odor of wintergreen and alcohol, came over with tears in his eyes.

'Gee, kid, that was great!' said the Babe. 'That was the greatest, kid!'

Lou, sitting in front of his famous locker Number 4, looked up and grinned at the Babe.

'That was for us,' he said quietly.

The Babe thought Lou meant a compact that he and Lou had made long ago about not competing for home-run honors. But it meant more than just the Babe and himself to Lou. It meant the host of others who had helped boost him from a janitor's son to the pinnacle of sports fame.

The story of Lou Gehrig is the retelling of the saga that America invented — the rise from rags to riches, from obscurity to fame, from nondescript to thoroughbred in one generation. In a way it is the story of the efforts of one man to better himself. But in its true sense it is the story of democracy: how one man can take to himself the hearts of many and justify the trust by a career above reproach.

Henry Louis Gehrig was born in New York on June 19, 1903. He lived with his father and mother in the upper eighties in the German section of Yorkville. His earliest recollection was that of one spring day when he entered the kitchen in response to a call from Christina Gehrig, his mother.

'Louie!' she called in German, peering into the cupboard that served as an ice-box. 'Louie, come. Mama wants you.'

The door swung open and Lou, a chubby, round-eyed youngster of four, stood waiting silently. Christina took a jar from the top shelf and dumped the contents into her palm. She counted out eight pennies and handed them to Lou.

'Mama wants you to go to the store and get a quart of milk,' she said.

'Quart of milk,' Lou repeated dutifully, also in German, and turned and departed.

Christina started the preparation of the family's meager evening meal. Only Louie and herself were home. Heinrich, her husband, was away on one of his frequent itinerant jobs. This time he was in Detroit, working as an automobile mechanic for the Simplex Company. Christina herself worked for a family downtown as a domestic, returning in time to clean and scrub their cramped quarters, and to get little Lou's supper.

Heinrich, like herself, had been born in Germany. He had rebelled at the rigid Prussian militaristic system that dominated the country, and when he was fourteen he had come to America to make his way. He had bummed his way around the country — riding the rods on freight cars, walking, hitching rides on farmers' wagons — usually working out his keep in his trade of tinsmith. At twenty-two he had married Christina.

Heinrich then settled, more or less, in New York, taking odd jobs whenever they were offered. Christina was willing to wait. She knew Heinrich was a young man and a foreigner. He had a lot to learn and the willingness to learn it. Perhaps this job in Detroit would lead to better things.

In the meantime she had to take care of Louie the best she could. Lou was her third child. The other two — a boy and a girl — had been sickly and died in infancy. But Lou howled so loudly when he was born that the doctor had told her he would live to be a lusty baby.

But where was he now? He should have been back from the store with the milk. He had been gone a long time.

'Louie!' called Christina again.

The door burst open and Lou ran weeping to his mother's arms, shaking with fright.

'What is it? What is it, Louie?' Christina pleaded, comforting him against her bosom. 'Tell mama what it is.'

'A man!' the boy sobbed, tears streaming down his face. 'A man. He made me look in a big black box.'

'Yes, and what was in the box?'

'I don't know. He just made me look into it and then he said I would have to pay him fifty cents.'

Even at four Lou knew that fifty cents was a good deal of money, more money than a quart of milk and a loaf of bread together would cost.

'Ach, we shall see what this is all about,' said

Christina stoutly. 'Come, Lou, show me the man.'
She took his chubby hand in hers and started out the
door leading to the street. Outside, she stopped. A
smile spread across her kindly face. The man stood
there on the sidewalk beside the box which had terri-
fied Lou.

'Louie, you must not be afraid,' she said gently.
'The man has taken your picture, that is all. Here,
we will see if it is good.' Turning to the photographer,
she held out her hand for the picture. 'See, Louie,
here is a picture of you. Isn't it nice? We will buy it,
and you must never be afraid of black boxes like this
again. Some day when you are a big man perhaps
you will look into big black boxes every day and
everybody will want a picture of you. But this one
we will keep for ourselves.'

The next year, when he was five years old, Lou was
sent to kindergarten, where he began to learn Eng-
lish. Then he was sent to P. S. 132 on Wadsworth
Avenue and 182d Street in upper Manhattan. Heinrich, who had hired out as a janitor when he first
came home from Detroit, got a job as an art-metal
mechanic. He was a leaf-hammerer, and hammered
designs in sheets of iron, bronze, and silver after they
had been marked by artists in regular patterns. He
did it well and soon was making excellent wages —
nearly thirty-five dollars a week. The Gehrigs moved
to a two-family apartment. This was the most ele-

gance they had ever known. There was a good deal of laughter about the home. Lou, years afterward, said, 'That's where I got the makings of the grin you fellows are always kidding me about.'

For the first time Christmas meant celebration. Lou listened excitedly to the tales his mother told him of the German Kris Kringle and American Santa Claus. On Christmas Eve he was quite willing to go to bed early when told that when he woke up there would be presents from Kris and Santa. But before morning Louie was awakened by an unusual thumping and bumping in the living-room. It was easily explained. His father had stopped at the corner for a few games of pinochle and a few glasses of beer before coming home with the gifts. His entrance had been anything but silent.

Lou awoke with a start upon hearing this noisy Santa and crept out of bed. Peering through the glass doors that separated the bedroom from the living-room, he stared wide-eyed. There were his father and his mother putting glass balls of every color on a fir tree and, on the floor, there were presents!

The next morning Lou identified the presents. They were a sled, a pair of rubber boots, and a catcher's glove — the first real Christmas presents he had ever received. It didn't matter that the catcher's glove was right-handed and Lou was left-handed, or that there was no snow and the sled couldn't be used on Christmas Day. It was all wonderful — even if Lou did know by now that there wasn't any Santa Claus.

When spring came, Lou took his catcher's glove and played baseball with the older kids in the neighborhood, in the lot just across the way at the corner of 102d Street and Second Avenue. They were older, for Lou was now only six, but they were not bigger. Louie was big and chunky and strong. Besides, he had a catcher's mitt, so Goose and Tony and Willie and Harold let him play with them and Lou — he loved it, even though he had to play with his beloved catcher's mitt on the wrong hand.

Like the rest he got up every morning at five o'clock and played until it was time to go to school. Sometimes they would glay games with other teams, each boy chipping in a penny or two to buy a 'Lively Bounder Ball,' which cost a quarter, with the winning team getting it when the game was over. If there was any money left, they would go to the near-by Fairbanks Bakery after the game, where, for ten cents, they could get all the stale cakes they could eat. Then they would go to the East River and swim and eat the cakes. In those days — 1909 — the East River was still a clean and pleasant place to swim.

Those were wonderful times, and little Lou made the most of them. His father was working regularly and his mother too. There was now always enough to eat and room enough in the apartment for all three to sleep at one time. There was a swimming hole and fellows to play ball with. The only fly in the ointment of Lou's life at the moment was Beanpole, the cop on the corner.

Fishcakes, the other cop, was swell. He would let Louie and Goose and Tony and the others even play with his nightstick. And if they were about to get into trouble he would tell them, just like a regular guy.

But Beanpole was different. He seemed to just go around trying to think up things to get mad about — little things like swiping empty sugar barrels and selling them to Hobson's warehouse, hooking potatoes with long pointed sticks out of the bins in the grocery store and roasting them in the woods, made Beanpole sore.

Nobody liked Beanpole at all. Many hours were spent just sitting around discussing ways and means to fix him. Many plans were suggested from time to time, some of which sent the gang into howls of laughter, but none proved practical when it came time for execution.

But one day Willie brought the news that they were going to take some movies right there in the neighborhood. It was in the old Pearl White thriller days of serials. The episode that was going to be shot,

the boys learned, was one of sending an automobile
crashing over the cliff into the East River with a
dummy tied inside.

Somehow, after the stunt was over, the youngsters
managed to steal the dummy. Carefully they lugged
it to the roof of a neighboring apartment house and
dangled it from a chimney with a rope around its
neck. They made sure it was in the corner farthest
from the roof trapdoor, then strung fine wires across
the roof at the height of a man's ankles.

Lou was chosen by lot to be the decoy. He rushed
down to the corner where the cop, Beanpole, was on
duty and screamed that a man had hanged himself on
the roof. Beanpole rushed up to the roof, while Lou
disappeared. The gang, hiding behind the chimneys
on another roof, got their revenge on Beanpole when
they saw him trip over the wires and take a header
onto the graveled tar of the roof.

That winter the gang forgot about cops in the excitement of sliding down Deep Grass Hill on Louie's
sled. Lou, now nearing his eighth birthday, liked to
sleigh-ride, but he was shy enough to refuse to go
whenever Goose's sister went along. He finally took
a long and hazardous ride by himself and managed to
get bruised up and the sled smashed up by crashing
into a fence-gate at the bottom of the hill.

Lou's exciting, energetic life made him grow and
flourish like a young bay tree. Each morning he

would get up and make his own breakfast — milk, toast, jam, and five or six eggs. Then he would carefully take seven pennies — no more — out of the now-famous cupboard jar and go to school. Those pennies would buy his lunch. When he came home, the first thing Louie would always do would be his homework. Then he would be bundled off to bed early — at least by seven-thirty — unless Heinrich and Christina decided that he had worked hard and deserved to go and see a local movie for ten cents.

School was Lou's most passionate interest outside of baseball. He was always among the top five in his class and never missed a day when he could help it — and he could always help it. On one occasion, when Louie was in 2–B grade, he became ill on Sunday. Christina called the doctor and he shook his head and said the boy had a fairly bad case of pneumonia. It was even worse the next day, but Lou watched his chances and when both Heinrich and Christina had gone to work, he got up, dressed, and went to school.

His teacher, however, discovered that he had a temperature and sent him up to Mr. Halligan, the principal. The principal quizzed the tearful Lou and discovered that the reason he had come to school was that he didn't want his attendance record broken. So Mr. Halligan solemnly promised Lou that if he went home and got back into bed, he would be marked 'present' for every day that his sickness kept him out. Lou agreed, and went home for two days.

Never in the years afterward did Lou Gehrig miss
a day at school. All during grade school, grammar
school, high school, and college, his attendance
record was unstained by one absence either from
playing hooky or from sickness. His grades were always either A's or B's.

Heinrich sometimes helped Lou with his sums.
Christina declared that his father got his mathe-
matics from his card-sense. He loved to play pinochle
in the corner saloon. One Friday night Heinrich
didn't come home from a pinochle game. Next morning when Christina and Lou were eating breakfast
they saw Heinrich come unsteadily up to the door.
As they watched they saw him stop and carefully ex-
tract a handful of crumpled bills from his pocket and
put them in his cap. Christina giggled but said nothing. When Heinrich was asleep she quietly rum-
maged in his cap and found seventeen dollars — the
fruits of her husband's winnings in the all-night
pinochle game.

'Come, Louie,' she said, her eyes twinkling. She
and Lou put on their best clothes, took the money,
and went to Coney Island. There they spent every
cent of the seventeen dollars on candy and hot-dogs,
rollercoasters and sideshows. When Heinrich found
out he swore off both beer and pinochle for two
weeks.

These escapades of his father made a deep impression on young Lou. He did not tolerate them the way Christina, his mother, did. He resented them and made up his mind never to drink himself.

Because Lou and his mother were together so constantly, the nine-year-old youngster was shy of other company beside the gang — especially girls. He used to play marbles with girls at 181st Street and Fort Washington Avenue; he even helped an Italian kid to steal marbles and sell them to the 'rich kids,' but when the gang began to grow up and introduced kissing games, Lou fled their company.

Nor was his shyness of people in general lessened by one incident that occured one Sunday night at a delicatessen. Christina had sent him to the corner to get some food for friends who had dropped in. Lou was dressed in his best suit and when he had made his purchases, including some eggs, turned to leave.

'Just a minute,' said the proprietor suspiciously, coming from behind the counter. 'I'm missing some candy.'

Lou, who had put his half-dozen eggs in one pocket, stood still. 'Search me,' he said with dignity. The proprietor slapped him on the hips and on the side pockets, breaking the eggs all over his new clothes.

Lou never forgot his embarrassment over that. But by the time he was eleven, in grade 7–A, he was getting accustomed to both girls and fame. He was beginning to be a locally famous athlete. The stocky

German boy with the chubby, rosy face and the pis-
ton-like legs was recruited to put the shot and to run
in the class hundred-yard relay. He also played baseball on the Oval Team, Park Department League,
100-pound class. The next year, when he was twelve,
his team won the city championship. Like nearly any
New York boy of those years of 1912–13, Lou idolized
such baseball heroes as Tris Speaker, Honus Wagner,
and George Burns. The Giants were his dream team,
McGraw his favorite character.

Not all of Lou's life was the small beer of school
and baseball skittles, however. He had got a job in a
delicatessen where he worked every afternoon. He
ran errands for neighborhood merchants, mowed
lawns in summer, and shoveled snow in winter. The
neighbors used to shake their heads: 'A strong back,
that Gehrig boy. Who knows about his brain?'

Christina had applied for and got a job at the
Sigma Nu fraternity house at Columbia University.
She was cook and housekeeper. Heinrich, in his off-
hours from leaf-hammering, took care of the furnace.
For several years following, Lou, now called the
'little Heinie' by the brothers in the Sigma Nu bond,
tossed ball bashfully with such a notable-to-be as
Bill Corum, New York *Journal-American* sports
columnist, attended school, got odd jobs such as collection boy at the New York Edison Company, and
went clamming on the mudflat and sold the clams to

Connor's Hotel. By this time the family was living on 112th Street in the best tradition of the New York rent migrant.

Three years later, the family was living at 15th Street and Irving Place in New York's Greenwich Village. Christina was working and commuting daily to Red Bank, New Jersey. Heinrich was still on his artisan's job and Lou — his name now having been shortened permanently to Lou — was entering the High School of Commerce at its 46th Street annex.

As usual, Lou's studies were excellent but his social attitude still gave him grief. His fellow-students kidded him because he still wore knee-breeches. Lou got a pair of long pants out of his part-time earnings and hid them in the dumb-waiter of the family's apartment. Each morning he would start for school in his knee-breeches. Downstairs he would haul down the dumb-waiter with the long pants, put them on over his short pants, and go to school. Coming home at night, Lou would doff the long pants, thrust them into the waiter, haul them up, and go upstairs again in his knee-breeches. This was one of the few times he deliberately deceived his mother, Christina. The agony of his shyness was too great to be overcome.

It was at the High School of Commerce that Lou Gehrig got his real start at the sport which was later to make him world-famous. Lou was hard at work on his main course of bookkeeping, keeping his nose to the grindstone and not going out for any extra-curricular sports at all. His ambition was eventually to be a civil engineer.

But Willie Contente, a friend of Lou's, told Coach Du Schatko, the Commerce baseball mentor, that there was a good ballplayer being wasted under the aegis of a C.P.A. Du Schatko asked Lou to report for baseball practice. Lou shook his head and explained that he had too much work to do. But Du Schatko, luckily for baseball history, was persistent. Finally he gave Lou a uniform and ordered him to report to the bench at a game in the Lewisohn Stadium.

Lou dubiously agreed to come. He started for the field with his nose buried in the bookkeeping text and went a station past his stop. He walked back, still studying, until suddenly the *moderato* roar of the high-school crowd came to his ear.

Lou stopped in horror. His shyness overwhelmed him. He turned on his heel and ran back home and the next day turned in his uniform. But Du Schatko's patience — and the threat of his bookkeeping teacher, who was a baseball enthusiast, to flunk him if he didn't play — finally won out. Lou became a member of the team and — for the records — took part in his first real ball game on a Saturday afternoon in May, 1917, at the age of fourteen. He played first base, and if he distinguished himself in any way the records do not show it.

Now Lou was really interested in sports in general and began to fit them willy-nilly into his daily schedule. In his junior year he played on the soccer team. He was seduced away from that part of the time to the football team by the wily Irish tongue of Buck O'Neill, the football coach, and went in at tackle for the varsity.

The day after he took up his position, Lou complained to O'Neill.

'I want to run with the ball,' he said.

'Get back in there,' ordered O'Neill.

Lou refused, saying that unless he could carry the ball he wouldn't play. O'Neill, outraged, ordered Lou to turn in his suit, which Lou willingly did and made ready to play soccer the next day.

O'Neill immediately wilted. Lou went into the backfield as fullback. That same fall he proved that his judgment was better than O'Neill's. In the crucial game of the season, although he had a broken boil on his nose — which, incidentally, virtually closed both Lou's eyes — the rotund Dutchboy, who had by now attained the weight of a hundred and eighty pounds, scored three touchdowns and kicked a goal from the 48-yard line.

Nor did Lou abate a jot from his strenuous schedule to get in his football playing during the next few years. Here is a sample of one day in those exciting school years: in the morning he served breakfast at the Alpha Chi Rho house, played soccer in a game won by 1 to 0, played football in a game which was won by 21 to 7, served seventy people at a tea and washed all the dishes, shoveled in twelve tons of coal from the sidewalk to the bin. Then Lou went to bed and slept a glorious twenty hours. He was only sixteen years old, and by now in his last year at the High School of Commerce.

But Lou's chief high-school glories, prophetically enough, came in baseball. Commerce had won the Police Athletic League championship in New York and was supposed to play Lane Technical at the Cubs' park in Chicago. It meant that Lou would have to be away from home for three days, and Christina set her foot down. She refused to let her Louie go so far away for so long. It took the personal persuasion of the new coach, Harry Kane, to make her let Lou go. He promised that Lou would be tucked in bed early, get good food, and return safe and sound.

Up to the time of the critical Chicago game, Lou's playing had been notably undistinguished. Never too well co-ordinated by nature, slow-thinking and solidly, rather than lithely, built, his fielding around first base had been less than spectacular. His throwing was good enough, but his batting was nothing extraordinary, something under .200 for three years.

Nevertheless, he went into the game. As Lou told

the story years afterward, the game went badly for Commerce. The score seesawed about until the ninth inning, when the board indicated that Commerce trailed, six runs to Lane Tech.'s eight runs. Two were out. It was the last half and Gehrig was coming to bat — and three men were on. At short-stop for Tech. was young Freddie Lindstrom, later to be the boy wonder of the New York Giants.

Lou, still trembling from his crowd-shyness, stopped in front of Kane. The coach's head was buried in his hands.

'Coach,' said Lou timidly. There was no response from the disconsolate Kane.

'Coach,' said Lou again, 'what'll I do?'

Kane looked up with a wild and hopeless gleam in his eye.

'Do?' he said in bitter sarcasm. 'Why, dig in your toes and hit it out of the park! That's what you've been doing all year, isn't it?'

Lou missed the sarcasm. He gulped down his heart and nodded. 'Yes, sir,' he said.

He waddled up to the plate and stood there waving his bat, a forlorn little fat boy in the midst of the great diamond and leveling rays of the sun. The exits were already crowded with jubilant Chicago high-schoolers, but they paused just to see what the fat boy from New York would do.

The pitcher threw the ball and it was a strike. He

wound up again, and Lou Gehrig, no longer trembling, suddenly lashed out with all the frenzied energy of a frustrated batting season. The bat cracked against the ball. The three runners, shrieking their joy, came home, one after the other and Lou, still watching the ball vanish into the bleachers of Cubs' park, jogged with a growing wonder, and confidence in his heart, around the bases. He heard the thunder of applause from the grandstand and for the first time in his life doffed his cap. He was no longer afraid, and the game was over: Commerce, 10; Lane Tech., 8.

In the showers after that schoolboy triumph, a little man came up to Lou and said he was a big-league scout for the Chicago Cubs. Lou had something he liked, he said; how about signing up an if-and-when contract? Lou laughed the little man out of the showers. The next day the Chicago papers ran Lou's picture next to that of the great Babe Ruth with the headline:

WILL THIS HIGH SCHOOL BOY BE THE NEXT
BABE?

Incidentally, for the record, there is another story about that epochal game. Lou's team-mates — who became businessmen in later life — say that Lou didn't win the game. He merely put it on ice. The score was 8 to 6 in favor of Commerce, and ended 12 to 6 after Lou's four-bag smash.

The next day Heinrich came in with news that seemed much more wonderful than Lou's home run to the Gehrigs. He said that he had a job for Lou during the summer. Lou was to be a tracer of designs for Caldwell's, the shop where his father was a leaf-hammerer, at the magnificent sum of eighteen dollars a week! To add to the overflowing cup, a friend of Lou's dropped in and said that they could try out for an acrobatic act at the German Turnverein that fall, just as Lou had always wanted.

The job never turned out very well. Lou did a competent stint, as it afterward proved, but his heart wasn't in it. He was dreaming of baseball and remembering the cheers of the crowd that had swept away all his youth complex of shyness. Nor did the Turnverein act prove much better. Lou's love was baseball. The testing of his affection was at hand.

Columbia Lou

IN 1920 Heinrich Louis Gehrig was going on his seventeenth birthday. He was a big-shouldered, big-calved, chunky youngster with a wide, bashful grin. He was ready to become a first-class tracer of designs for leaf-hammerers and had forgotten that he had ever pumped a home run for Commerce High School or that a scout for the Cubs had talked to him of playing big-league baseball.

But in 1920 Fate put a finger on his shoulder. His father Heinrich fell seriously ill. The burden of supporting his father and himself fell wholly on Christina, his mother. Lou wanted to quit school immediately, but his mother insisted that he finish his education. So Lou entered Columbia University, principally because the athletic director of the university was the same man who had managed the Sigma Nu house when Christina had worked there. Lou remembered his kindness — and the fact that he was also of German stock — and immediately decided on Columbia as his *alma mater*.

He was not ready to take the Columbia entrance examinations, but six months of cramming at the Extension School got him by with flying colors, to begin a B.S. course in preparation for engineering. But it was only after long hours of night study and brain-wearying. He pounded the facts in his book into his brain with the same grim pertinacity that he put into everything — even his hair-combing. Lou never got anything the easy way.

Lou continued to cram during his two years at Columbia and made surprisingly good marks, considering all the burdens he carried on his brawny shoulders. He also went in for athletics as much as he could. But he never let them interfere with an assortment of spare jobs on and off the Columbia campus. He always dressed in baggy old pants and a white shirt, sometimes with a gray sweatshirt on top. No coat ever covered his shoulders, nor did he ever wear a hat on his wavy brown hair even in the depths of winter. His face was always ruddy and cheerful, with a grin for everybody he passed no matter whether he knew them or not. He was still the 'fat boy' of his Yorkville days, but a good deal of the fat was now muscle.

He played right tackle for the Columbia Lions with

a degree of fame. He was not quick or able at diagnosing plays, but it was a saying at Columbia that no one could get through Lou's corner at tackle unless Lou were dead — 'and he's damn far from dead,' the saying used to end. In baseball Lou was shunted around for some time as he had been at Commerce. First he played in the outfield, where he made a mess of catching balls. Then he was put in as pitcher, where he was wild enough nearly to decapitate some of the best players on the Columbia team, as he jokingly put it years later. He once struck out seventeen men in a game but lost, 7 to 1, because he walked virtually all the others. Lou settled down at first base, where all he had to do was scoop in the balls that were thrown at him.

His fielding was erratic, but his hitting had gradually improved by constant practice. Now it reached the point where it was phenomenal. Lou began whacking out extra base hits on Columbia's South Field, each one getting longer and longer until he had smashed seven home runs in two years. One of these is said to be the longest ball ever hit on the field. It went more than four hundred and twenty-five feet, and would have probably sailed a good deal farther except that it shattered a window in the School of Journalism. Any Columbia graduate who has played ball on South Field will swear that such hitting is great hitting.

Coach Carriss of Pennsylvania called Lou the best player to come out of college since Sisler. New York papers sat up on the sports pages and called him 'Columbia Babe.' Rumors began to seep through that year of 1923 that Lou had been offered a berth with the New York Yankees, who needed a replacement at first base to bolster up the great but aging Wally Pipp.

Lou laughed off the rumors. He refused to discuss them even with the *bona fide* representatives of the big-league teams who approached him. But he knew that his father needed an operation badly and that his mother and himself, with his off-time income, could not provide the money. They struggled along until late in 1923, when Christina fell sick for the first time in her life with double pneumonia. Lou had to get some money fast — some big money.

The Athletics had been after him to sign up. So had the Washington scouts, and six other major-league teams. Lou himself had been a Giant fan until he had seen the famous Babe clout one one day. Now he idolized the Yankees above all other teams. He was offered fifteen hundred dollars bonus by Colonel Ruppert, the Yankee owner, if he would join up with them and three thousand dollars a year.

Lou went home and told his mother that he had decided to quit Columbia and join the Yanks. Christina, for one of the few times in her life, broke down and cried. She had her heart set on her son's going through college and becoming a certified public accountant or an engineer.

'I'll be well again soon,' she said, 'and then everything will be all right.'

For two days Lou tried to convince her of his side of the argument — which was simply that signing a baseball contract would give them all the necessary money they needed.

Heinrich Gehrig also objected: 'I don't want a dummer for a son.'

But at last Christina gave in. Lou went back to the Phi Delta Theta house where he roomed, said good-bye to the boys, packed his paper suitcase with his few clothes, and left.

He knew where to go. The week-end before he had pitched for Columbia, in one of his rare stands off first base, and won the game against New York University, 7 to 2. He got three hits that day, including one home run over the fence.

In the showers — where it seems most of the important business matters of Gehrig's life were settled — Lou was approached by a short, fat little man.

'My name's Krichell,' he said curtly. 'Come down to the office Monday and talk things over.'

Lou, dazed, said nothing. But he saw Andy Coakley, the Columbia coach, nodding at him.

'Y-yes, sure,' stammered Columbia Lou, swabbing himself with soap. Krichell turned and went out.

'Who was that?' demanded Lou of Coakley.

'That was Paul Krichell,' shouted Coakley, dashing into the shower long enough to slap Lou on his wet back. 'The Yankees want us to sign up!'

So the first place Lou went was to Andy Coakley's on Monday and then to the Yankee office. The contract was signed and Lou was told to report to the park next day. Lou went right home and waved the contract in front of Christina's still dubious eyes.

'Here,' said Lou, shaking a check, 'is the money for papa's operation!'

So it was. The first money from his signing check went to put Heinrich Gehrig on the operation table and, as the doctors later said, to save his life.

Lou was nervous, however, the next day. The ordeal of going to the Yankee clubhouse and facing all the famous players that he had heretofore only seen at a distance on the field left him sweating and weak. So he pressed Andy Coakley into service again and they went down to the clubhouse together.

'I've been in college gyms before,' said Lou, fidgeting, 'and I've been in these semi-pro clubhouses over in Jersey. I didn't tell you, Andy, but I used to get some extra dough over there playing ball under the name of Long.'

Andy grinned.

'That's all right, kid,' he said.

'But this will be different, won't it?' asked Lou earnestly.

Andy shook his head.

'Not so much, kid,' he replied easily. 'Not so much.'

When they walked into the clubhouse that afternoon, all of the famous Yankees team of 1923 was there, most of the team that was first to make the legend of Murderers' Row a reality. Some were half-dressed and joshing. Over in one corner, Joe Bush, the pitcher of bullet-ball fame, Bob Meusel, the peerless outfielder, Aaron Ward, and the first holder of the longevity record on the baseball field, Deacon Everett Scott, the Yankee short-stop, were playing cards.

But right next to the door was the great Babe Ruth himself, half-dressed and oiling his glove. There was no mistaking the rotund beaming face, spindleshanks, and heavy-set body.

Lou stared at everybody but no one noticed him. Some of the players looked up at Coakley and said, 'Hello, Andy,' but no one paid any attention to the lumbering boy alongside him.

'Come along,' said Andy Coakley, shaking Lou gently. They went into the inner sanctum, the office of Miller Huggins, the famous little pilot of the Yanks.

Hug was sitting at his desk, his heels upon it, staring into space.

'Hello, Hug,' said Andy. 'This is the young guy from Columbia I was telling you about.'

Without taking his feet from the desk, Huggins swiveled his little dark eyes and concentrated their stare on Lou.

'Hello, Gehrig,' he said. 'Tell Woodie to give you a uniform.' Woodie was the Yankee trainer.

He said nothing more to Lou. Instead, he turned to Coakley.

'Hmm,' he said slowly. 'He sure is a big guy. Is he Jewish?' Huggins had his eye eternally on the box office, and a good Jewish ballplayer — or an Italian ballplayer — has always been the acme of a big-league manager's idea of a box-office draw.

'No,' said Andy. 'He's German.'

Huggins seemed a little disappointed, but he brightened.

'That's all right,' he said. 'That'll do fine. That's almost as good as Jewish.'

Gehrig went out into the dressing-room, got his uniform from Woodie, and put it on. He felt curiously alone and a stranger.

He said afterward that he felt as a friend of his must have felt on the day he graduated from college. Lou reported that his friend came into the Phi Delta house still wearing his mortarboard and black gown, with the rolled diploma in his hand. He sat down in a chair, threw one leg over the arm, and pushed the board back.

'Well,' he said, waving the diploma, 'now that I've

got it, what am I going to do with it?' The same
question popped up in Lou's mind. He was on the
Yankee team now — what was he going to do about
it?

Lou found out. He warmed the bench. He watched
the other players. He pitched in the bull-pen. He
shagged flies, hit fungoes. He did everything but
play in a game.

The newness of being with the Yankees began to
wear off. Lou, who really believed that he was not
earning his salary, began to fret, but he was too shy
to say anything to Huggins about it — and besides,
he still held the little manager in awe.

Late that same fall, after warming the bench in
his new uniform for what seemed endless weeks,
Huggins beckoned to him during a game with Washington. 'Get up there and take a cut out of the ball,'
he ordered Gehrig. Lou was to hit for the pitcher.

Lou was shaking as he selected his bat, trembling
as he stepped into the box, fairly vibrating as the
announcer gave his name over the public-address
system for the first time in big-league ball.

Hollingsworth, a fair-to-middling pitcher, was
pouring them in for the Senators. He had one good
pitch — a fast ball with a sweeping overhand delivery. He wound up and sent the ball across the plate.
Lou swung and missed. Hollingsworth wound up
again. Lou swung — and missed. Again Hollings-

worth burned the ball in. Lou swung — and missed. The pride of Columbia on his first trip to the plate had struck out on three pitched balls.

Lou turned and walked back to the bench, dragging his bat beside him. The walk seemed miles long. Worst of all, when he sat down on the bench, the only seat vacant was that next to his idol — Babe Ruth.

But for the first time the Babe seemed to see him. He grinned in that famous boyish way of his and gave Lou a single hearty pat.

'Never you mind, kid,' he boomed. 'You'll pickle one next time. You took your cuts anyway. You didn't just stand there and watch the balls go by.'

Lou never appreciated anything more in his life. The quick tears stung his eyes. He had been so sure that his muffing that chance would mean the end of his career in organized baseball. He choked up and couldn't speak a word in reply.

The Babe's words were prophetic. Huggins let Lou simmer a few days before he sent him in to hit again. This time the big youngster — whose face the sports writers were already beginning to describe as 'that classic collar-ad pan' and whose general physique was, in the words of the *Times's* John Kieran, marked with 'the slim, delicate lines of a railroad locomotive' — was grimly determined to show everybody, including himself.

The Yanks were playing St. Louis. Elam Van Gilder, a seasoned old-timer, was pitching. There was a runner on second and Huggins sent Lou up to the plate.

Van Gilder sent just the kind of ball that Hollingsworth had served up — a sizzling pitch across the heart of the plate. The news that the big green kid named Gehrig was a sucker for a fast, straight ball had got around the major-league grapevine.

Lou gritted his teeth, dug in his spikes, and swung from the heels. His whole body relaxed in thankfulness as he heard the sharp smack and felt the twinge in his fingers on the bat-handle that indicated the ball had been hard and cleanly hit.

The ball bounced off the right-field fence in a line drive for a double. The runner came home and Lou slid into second. As he picked himself up and dusted himself off, he said aloud, 'Well, that's one they can't kid me about.'

No one did kid him. Instead, Huggins got up from his seat when Lou came in and gave him the final accolade: 'Nice hitting, kid!' The Babe grinned and nodded wisely. Ever since then, Van Gilder was Lou's favorite pitcher — more than once he smacked him for safeties, more than once Van Gilder struck him out. But ever afterward, Lou liked to play in a game where he batted against Van Gilder.

Not everything went as smoothly as that, but the

Babe was always on Lou's side. When Lou started his first big-league game with the Yanks in 1923 it was again against Washington. Bullet Joe Bush was pitching that day and Huggins told the players in the clubhouse that Lou would play first base.

'Hell,' complained Joe, 'that kid doesn't know what it's all about, Hug. He'll boot the game away.' Joe had had a good year and he wanted to win this particular game.

'Aw,' said the Babe jokingly, 'let him play, Joe. Maybe he'll sock one on the nose and win your game for you.'

Lou started at first base. In the fourth inning Lou had made no glaring misplays, but he was walking on pins and needles. The score was still 0 to 0. Sam Rice was on third base, Bucky Harris was on first, and Joe Judge was at bat.

Joe, a smart ballplayer if there ever was one, did exactly the right thing calculated to confuse a rookie. He laid down a perfect bunt on the first-base line toward Lou for a squeeze play. Lou came pounding in and fielded the ball perfectly — and then didn't know what to do with it. He stood there with the ball in his glove, paralyzed, while Rice tore across home plate, Harris slid into second in a cloud of dust, and Judge passed him on the baseline like a summer typhoon. All the runners were safe.

Joe Bush tore off his cap and stamped on it. He

raised his fists to heaven and hollered. Then he approached Lou.

'Whatsa matter, stupid?' he snarled. 'Got molasses on your fingers? Is the ball stuck? Got frozen brains? Is that how they teach you to think at college?'

Lou moved away dumbly. He said nothing to Bush and the game went on. But in his heart he was preparing for his moment. It came in the seventh inning.

Lou came up with the bases full and his usually smiling mouth compressed into a grim line that boded no good for the Washington pitcher. A moment later he had pasted a double into center field, scored three runs, and won the game for Bush.

At the end of the inning, Bullet Joe waited for him. They walked across the diamond together, Joe's arm around Lou's neck.

'I'll say this for you, kid,' Joe said finally. 'You're dumb but you can sure smack the apple. What you need is to get out there and practice, practice, practice. And thanks for the game.'

Lou didn't think much of the advice then, but the next day Bush insisted on getting him out on the diamond before practice. He bunted to Lou until the sweat streamed down his body. Bush cursed and yelled, but every minute Lou learned a new angle about playing first base.

Huggins, out watching the two at practice, turned to one of the writers and said:

'He's going to be a great ballplayer, that kid Gehrig. When he came here he didn't know a thing, he was one of the dumbest players I've ever seen. But he's got one great virtue that will make him: he never makes the same mistake twice. He makes all the mistakes, all right, but not twice. He may make three errors today, but tomorrow he'll make one a day. Then it'll be one every other day, then one a week, then one a month. And finally he'll be a great ballplayer.'

For all time, according to Lou, those were the most apt truths that anyone ever said about him.

As he worked out his faults, Lou made more friends. One of the first was his boyhood idol, Tris Speaker. In the summer of 1923 he made his first trip around the circuit and the first stop was Cleveland. Lou saw the great Speaker with his graying hair talking to Babe Ruth, and began edging up to them like a kid looking for an autograph. The Babe noticed him and beckoned him over.

'What's the matter, kid?' he asked genially. 'Scared of this old leatherneck?'

Spoke — as they called him — just grinned.

'Hear you're the kid that's going to make Swiss cheese out of the Babe's record,' he said. 'I hope you do. He's getting too fresh.'

A little later, Lou smacked a line drive in batting practice that hit the right-field wall in the Cleveland Park and bounded back almost to the infield

'Nice hitting!' yelled Spoke. 'Keep it up.'

Another friend of Lou's was Eddie Collins, the soft-spoken second-baseman of the White Sox. He was a college man himself from Columbia and made it a point to look Lou up. Eddie always had the idea that the more college men took up major-league baseball the better it would be. He advised Lou that playing the game was just like taking a college course — that there was a lot to learn and it couldn't all be done by a season's cramming.

Lou found out that Eddie Collins was right that same year. In August, 1923, Huggins called him into the office and told him that he was being farmed out to the Hartford Club of the Eastern League. Lou went out of the Yankee front office with every roseate dream shattered. If someone had offered him any kind of job at that moment he would have taken it. But nobody did, and Lou went disconsolately off to the Hartford Club.

Immediately the character of his baseball life changed. Where, at the Yankees, he had been sitting on the bench week in and week out, now he was playing every day — and playing badly. His whole gloomy mental attitude threw him into a slump. He could neither field nor hit. Pat O'Connor, the Hartford manager, was in a hole. He was ready to crate Lou and send him back to the Yanks when one day Gehrig hoisted a home run over the wall and broke up the game.

Then Pat's attitude to Lou changed. He began coaching the big fellow on handling himself and drilling in bits of information about inside baseball tactics. The two of them held secret skull sessions every day.

The best bit of advice Pat gave him was to make baseball his business.

'It's only a five-month season,' said Pat. 'Put your heart into it and save your parties for the winter's six months. You can't ride a horse two ways — you can't go to parties at night and play good ball in the daytime.'

Lou treasured that advice and added to it a tidbit which the Babe passed on to him after long experience.

'Don't be a sucker, kid,' the Babe told him. 'Keep in condition. Look at me: I made a lot of mistakes, I didn't live right, I didn't eat right and I had to pay for all those mistakes later on. You take a tip from me and tell the party guys to go sell their papers.'

Lou always remembered that advice and kept in the top of condition. He rarely went on parties and almost never drank or smoked. Occasionally he would take a glass of beer. In those early days with the Yanks he went over to a saloon with George Pipgras to have a drink and saw a few of the Yankees — Meusel, the Babe, and Combs — having a beer. Gehrig bolted back to the clubhouse, and when Pipgras found him he was packing his suitcase.

'Gee, George,' said Lou abashedly. 'I saw all those fellows there, but I was so scared when I saw them that I thought sure I would get fired for being there.'

Pipgras convinced him of his mistake, but Lou always afterward regarded beer with suspicion. He only took a cocktail to be a good fellow, and then one was the limit of his drinking.

As for conditioning, Lou was always a model. Starting at Hartford, he used to go to the park before the game and practice up on his fielding on every possible kind of ball from a bunt to a foul to a line drive under the tutelage of O'Connor. He practiced at three positions — as left-handed pitcher, left-handed hitter, and left-handed baseman.

His hitting soon began to be the chief topic of conversation in Hartford.

Following his début with a home run, Lou started running wild. He celebrated his twenty-first birthday by breaking the world's record for consecutive home runs, hitting seven in seven days, the seventeenth of the season.

'Gehrig owns Hartford now,' wrote an enthusiastic sports scribe.

Lou was to spend two years in the Eastern League with occasional visits back to the Yanks, and during that time the big, six-foot, one-inch, bashful fellow became the town hero. Up until June 8, 1924, for example, Lou had pitched nine games, won six, and had batted .491. On July of the same year he hit his twenty-seventh home run, had smashed out three home runs in one game, and his batting average was .390.

The fans adoringly dubbed him 'Columbia Lou Gehrig.' The consensus was that Fence-Breakin' Lou from Columbia could 'hit a bad ball further than most ballplayers could hit a good one.'

Lou ended the 1924 season with thirty-seven home runs. As a matter of record his career with the Hartford Club in the Eastern League bushes under the kindly tutelage of red-faced Pat O'Connor was over. The Yankees needed a first baseman to replace the creaky Wally Pipp. The foresight of Miller Huggins was justified, and at the beginning of the 1925 training season Lou Gehrig was told to report to St. Petersburg, Florida, the Yankee training camp. He was due to become a regular on the most famous team in baseball.

Not everyone thought Lou would be a great ballplayer in those remote days.

'He'll never last,' said Ty Cobb contemptuously of Lou when he came back to the big leagues after his triumphal exit from the Connecticut bushes. 'Look at those piano legs.'

In all fairness, though, it should be recorded that Cobb said the same thing of Babe Ruth with the same intonation but with a single word changed:

'He'll never last. Look at those *spindle* legs.'

Ty's remark might better have been applied to the Yankees in the spring of 1925. When Lou joined them they were far from a world's-champion aggregation. The club had been dredging up the bottom of the American League, getting trounced soundly by virtually every other team, again and again.

To Lou, who had come back from Hartford full of zip from his hitting triumphs, the team was a little disappointing. He remembered the old gang of 1923, and their winning ways. The regulars were almost the same now. Deacon Everett Scott at short-stop, the equable and ever-present grand tactician with the careful manners and padded shoes; Jumping Joe Dugan at the hot corner of third, specializing on making double plays out of whistling line drives; Waite Hoyt, the scholarly southpaw who knew his Shakespeare at least as well as a high-school junior; Bob Shawkey, almost as mighty a pitcher as he was a hunter, telling yarns of baseball prowess and deer-hunting in the same breath; Wallie Pipp, the error-less first baseman, who indulged in long, intricate-sounding discussions on finance with Miller Huggins; Ernie Johnson, the slugging utility outfielder and his omnivorous yen for a game of bridge; Herb Pennock of the baffling delivery and hunt-club lingo, whose chief diversion, he always claimed, was riding to hounds; Wallie Schang, the great catcher who was

the baldheaded Great Wall of China when it came
to blocking a run; the soft-voiced, taciturn Bob
Meusel and Earl Combs, both full of wisdom and the
knowledge of how to play ball in the outfield and how
to make Texas Leaguers at bat; the fleet Whitey Witt,
and, of course, the Babe, always bubbling with card-
talk and endless discussions of his proposed chicken
farm.

All these had been heroes in the eyes of a raw recruit. Now, in the eyes of Lou returning after two
years-odd of seasoning, many of them seemed a little
worn and tired. And although the glamour of the
great Yankees had not left the club enough to dim
their work on the field and at bat — their present
standing was generally looked upon as an understand-
able slump after years of top-notch ball — most of
them were over-age destroyers by baseball standards.

Most of all Wallie Pipp had changed. Back in 1923
he had had his best year. His deep-pocketed glove
snared everything that came within twenty feet of
the first sack and he, as Lou later said, 'was hitting
with the best in the business.'

Lou had learned most of his first-base lore merely
by watching Pipp in those days, seeing how to shift
his feet (the Yanks called Lou 'Tanglefoot' for a long
time), how to save inches on a put-out or throw, how
to cover up and make plays to second or home, how
to make double plays, how to go down on a foul or
bunt, what tricks to use on individual batters.

In those days, Lou had simply despaired of ever getting a place on the Yanks.

'They're too good,' he used to mutter to himself. 'I'll never break in.'

He hadn't realized that Time works on the side of the young. Now Wallie was playing without the fire that had characterized him in 1923. He was still sure in his plays but, around first base at least, the Yankees showed symptoms of slowing up.

Miller Huggins didn't seem to notice it. If he did, he didn't seem to worry. Day after day the same combination went in and Lou slid restlessly back and forth on the Yankee bench, wearing out three sets of uniform trousers. Apparently he was doomed to stay there for quite a while longer.

But his tenure on the bench was already fairly insecure. One sports-writer noted:

> Lou Gehrig is back with the Yankees. There is a reason for it. Five other clubs in the American League refused to waive on him last year. Should Manager Huggins try the same maneuver again, there would probably be more. It is tough on Huggins, as Lou is a first baseman and Wallie Pipp refuses to get old. Should Gehrig be able to hit major-league pitching he may get a place in the outfield....

Gehrig thought he could hit major-league pitching. He knew what George Burns, one of his boyhood idols who played first base for Boston, had said about him only a year back when Gehrig had batted a few times for the Yanks in a game against the Red Sox. According to Tom Connolly, chief of the American League umpires, the first time up, Gehrig hit the ball a mile. The next time he hit it a mile and a quarter. The third time he drove it a mile and a half. As he rounded first base, Burns said: 'That guy a college guy? Hell, no! That hitting son-of-a-gun is a blacksmith!'

And Lou had some of the confidence that had, once upon a time back in his Columbia days, caused old Uncle Wilbert Robinson of the Brooklyn Dodgers to swoon away. Uncle Robbie was mildly interested in Lou at the time and inquired just how much the big-shouldered guy would ask to sign up.

Lou sent the same answer that he had given to Krichell, and rotund Uncle Robbie staggered and fell in a faint on the Brooklyn clubhouse floor, making a sizable dent in the concrete.

'Fifteen hundred dollars?' gasped Uncle Robbie. 'A college kid like that wants fifteen hundred dollars? He ought to be glad to play for nothing! Send him right back to college!' All of which fazed Lou not at all in his demands.

So Lou decided, not without much mental torture, to take the final jump with Miller Huggins. One day in late May, 1925, after the game — it was in Chicago — Lou came to the crossroads. He decided to tackle Hug in person.

After dinner he went to look Hug up, but the little man was out to a play. Lou took a seat in the hotel lobby and stuck there. The hours passed, his bedtime of nine o'clock came and went, and still he waited, glued to the seat of his leather easy chair. The other players came in, went upstairs, and to bed. But Lou stuck.

Finally, at midnight, Hug arrived. He saw Lou sitting in the deserted lobby and he stopped short and stared. It was the first time the big fellow had even come close to breaking training. Huggins's lips tightened and he walked ominously across toward Lou.

But Gehrig beat him to the verbal punch. He got up and said without preamble:

'I hear you're getting Mark Koenig from St. Paul for short.'

Huggins nodded, still mute with rage.

'I hear you're sending a couple of players up there in exchange for him.'

Hug, stunned, nodded again.

Lou went on determinedly:

'Well, I would like to be one of those players. I want to play ball. I *can* play ball. I'm sick of sitting on the bench doing nothing. I want a job I can work at.'

Huggins's wrath vanished. He began to grin. He patted Lou on the shoulder, standing on tiptoe to do it.

'Come upstairs with me, kid,' he said.

Lou followed him to his room, where Hug began packing for his trip, talking between tossing shirts and socks into his bag.

'Listen, Lou,' Huggins said. 'I'd like to send you out of the league but I can't get waivers on you. I know how you feel. I went through the same thing when I was a green kid breaking in and it's mighty discouraging. But let me tell you this — you have a good chance to make a big-league grade. You're not good enough though, yet. You're green and you've got a lot to learn. Some I'll teach you, some you'll learn yourself.'

Hug turned around and gestured with a shoe-tree.

'You think you can play ball better than some of the boys on the field — Pipp, for example. I've been watching you, and I know. But you can't play as well as Pipp — yet. You're not seasoned enough. Just go back to the bench, keep your mouth shut and your eyes and ears open. Your chance will come.'

With a friendly push toward the door, Huggins indicated to Lou that the talk was over.

'Get a good sleep and don't worry, young fellow,' he said at the door. 'I promise you everything will be all right.'

Lou understood. Such talk and such a promise from Huggins were better guarantees than government bonds. He went back to sliding up and down the bench, satisfied to learn as hard as he could and wait out his turn. And the time came.

◐

Buster Lou

JUNE 2, 1925, Wallie Pipp was up in batting practice.
The batting pitcher was named Caldwell, a Princeton
tryout, who was on trial with the Yanks. Over-eager
to show off, Caldwell shot over a fast, wild inshoot.
It caught Pipp on the side of the head. Wallie insisted he was all right — though they had to carry
him into the clubhouse.

Miller Huggins was doubtful. When he saw Pipp
gulp a couple of aspirins, he was sure.

He called Lou into his office.

'You're going in to play for Wallie,' he said abruptly. 'He's been hitting around .240. I want you
to do better. And for God's sake keep those big feet
out of your way.'

Suddenly the room was a bright mist to Lou. He
turned uncertainly around, pounding the pocket of
his mitt in growing excitement. He was on his way
out when Huggins called him back.

'Listen, Lou,' he said in a more kindly tone. 'I'm putting you in regularly if you make good. Don't let me down. And don't get worried if you boot one, and don't get excited. Do the best you can.'

Lou said nothing. He couldn't get the words past the lump in his throat. He just turned and rushed out to the dugout.

Actually, however, Lou's great string of consecutive games played did not start on the records that day. It had begun officially the day before when Lou was sent in to bat for Peewee Wanninger in the eighth inning. Lou had flied out to Goose Goslin in the Washington outfield. It was a technical beginning, but it counted in the scorebooks. It was overlooked for several years until Lou himself pointed it out.

Ironically enough, Wanninger was the man who had been sent in by Miller Huggins on May 6 to break the consecutive string of Deacon Scott's 1307 successive games played, a record that Lou was later far to surpass.

Deacon Scott had been very attentive about that record. On one occasion he was barred from the field by a painful outbreak of boils, but it rained and he kept his record intact. Another time a train wreck delayed his getting to the game until the seventh inning, but he made it anyway by a bit of hitch-hiking and fast running.

Lou had seen the Deacon toss his glove in to the

bench. He had both envied his record and was sorry
for the fact of his benching. He did not know that
one day the same performance would be held, this
time with Lou himself holding the record and turning
in his glove, with the Deacon in the grandstand,
watching.

The records do not indicate that Lou did anything
to startle the keepers of statistics on his first day.
But a yellowed newspaper clipping which Lou always
carried in his wallet indicated that on that day in the
Stadium against Washington Lou collected one
double and two singles, helping end the losing streak
of the year of the Yanks, who won 8 to 5.

Gehrig played one hundred and twenty-six games
that year. But he was still something of a stum-
blebum around first base, likely to get rattled in an
emergency. He was easily confused on a fast play.
Yet he could smash a ball from his shoe tops and he
would try for every ball near him. And he was true
to Huggins's first idea of him — that he never made a
mistake twice. His essential lack of conceit made him
an apt pupil of all the other Yankees who would teach.

The foremost of Lou's tutors was the Babe himself,
who had taken kindly to Lou from the first.

Lou used to watch the Babe day after day, seeing
the perfect timing and rhythm of his hitting, how the
big man managed to get every ounce of his weight
behind the blow without losing a drop of his smooth-

ness. Lou always maintained that Cobb and Speaker might be good hitters but that Babe Ruth was the tops. Up until the time he saw Babe in action he had been a 'choke' hitter — grabbing the bat inches from its end. Now Lou slid his grip right down to the handle-end and took a full, fast cut at the ball with his huge shoulders and more than two hundred pounds behind every blow.

The Babe tipped him to one of his own favorite stunts.

'You got to learn how to hit to right if you're gonna hit home runs,' said the Bambino. 'Take a tip from me. You hit to left and center most of the time. Pull your hits to that short right field that most American League ball parks have and most of those long put-outs, doubles, and triples will be home runs.'

Lou worked on that angle a long time, but he never did perfect it. What stymied him was the fact that he couldn't lift the ball into the air very often. Most of Lou's hits were line drives. Somebody counted one hundred and thirty such drives in his first full season at ball. Twenty-one happened to be home runs.

Tips on fielding came from everywhere. Vitally helpful was his surreptitious study of George Sisler, one of the greats of all time. Lou especially used to wish he could shift his feet the way Sisler did. Another helping hand came from Ernie Johnson; another, of course, from Miller Huggins.

'Just like a father to me,' said Lou.

Lou did his best and sometimes nearly died trying. He would pursue a ball anywhere, down dugout steps, into field boxes, up against concrete walls, with all the vim and do-or-die spirit of a Rutgers undergraduate. He made put-outs at all the bases, including the home plate. Many a time the official scorers have scratched their heads at the sight of Gehrig turning up from nowhere behind third base to cut off a throw and a runner.

Lou's cut-offs weren't uniformly successful, however. In one game against Detroit, a man was racing home and the Babe made a long throw-in from right field. The ball was coming in on a line and it had a fifty-fifty chance of getting to the plate with the runner. But Lou eagerly cut it off and then stood dazed with the ball in his mitt. He just couldn't keep hands off the horsehide if it was anywhere near him.

The other lessons Lou had to learn on the ball-field were the lessons of how to get along with officials in baseball. Ordinarily unostentatious and extremely friendly and willing, Lou sometimes found obstacles that even his good nature couldn't surmount. He had no answer, for example, to an angry charge from John McGraw of the Giants that he was a 'contract-jumper.' Lou had simply worked out with the Giants at the Polo Grounds in 1923 and had made no contract, but McGraw was sore at losing a good man.

There is the story that Lou did play at Hartford
for the Giants under the name of 'Lou Lewis.' According to the story, after Lou worked out with the
Giants at the Polo Grounds, he was taken in to see
McGraw. The crusty leader of the New York team
ordered him to Hartford for seasoning.

Then, continues the story, Lou made a miserable
showing both in the field and at bat. He was about
ready to give up when the news came that the manager of the Hartford team had committed suicide by
jumping overboard from a Fall River boat.

That settled Lou. He packed and returned to New
York.

This much is certain: Lou never had a contract
with the Giants which he considered valid and they
never pressed any interest they might have had in
him.

Umpires only bothered Lou once — at Cleveland.
Lou was in the coaching box at first and Ward, a
Yankee outfielder, hit a long drive near the foul line.
Billy Evans, the umpire, called it foul. Lou ranted —
an unusual thing for him to do — and said it was fair
in no uncertain terms.

Billy heard him out, then jerked his thumb.
'You're through, kid,' he said. Lou raised his voice
again and described Billy in direct terms as a blind
bat that had no right to be hanging around decent
baseball games, also as the left-handed whelp of a
mole.

'Are you finished?' said Billy calmly. Lou nodded belligerently.

'Then take a walk,' said Billy. 'That will cost you one hundred dollars just to make you remember that in this league an umpire's decision is final.'

Lou's stomach turned over. A hundred dollars was an awful lot to him yet. But Benny Bengough, his room-mate, and the Yankees' regular catcher, was standing near-by.

'Aw, Billy,' he said. 'You can't clip the kid that much. That's four weeks' pay.'

Billy Evans grinned.

'All right,' he said. 'The fine's off. But chase yourself, Lou. You're too excited to see this man's game.'

Lou hardly ever got into another major fuss with an umpire. In fact, he stayed so far away that a few years later President Ban Johnson of the American League singled him out as a great example to the youth of America — because he caused umpires no trouble. Lou could have told him that the strings that tied his purse also tied his tongue.

It was always Lou's argument, however, that not half so many players argued with the umpires as seemed to. The fans, he always declared, simply got the wrong impression. As an example, he cited an 'argument' Babe Ruth had with Clarence Rowland at the Stadium one day. The pitcher had whizzed

one over the pan and Babe had turned and said something to Rowland, who had called it a strike.

Immediately the stands were in pandemonium,
thinking that the Babe was complaining. As a matter
of fact the Babe had turned to Rowland with a look
of wonder on his face and said:

'Holy mackerel, Clarence, did you see that one
break? That fellow never showed me a hook like that
before. Where did he get that one?'

Lou got along with everyone on the other teams
with the exception of Ty Cobb. Ty never liked Lou
in the early days. Lou was just what Cobb thought a
ballplayer ought not to be: meek, inoffensive, a slugger, a big guy, a rube. So whenever the Yanks played
Detroit, Ty would razz Gehrig by calling him a
'thick-headed Dutchman... a satchel-footed rube
... a hunk of wiener schnitzel.'

Once in a tight game with Detroit, Lou got a clean
single in a pinch, but by dumb base-running managed
to get down between first and second.

'You big Dutchman,' snarled Cobb as he thrust the
ball with unnecessary violence between Lou's shoulder blades. 'You ain't got the guts to run the bases.'

The running fire of vituperative jockeying kept up
from the dugout. At last a muttered crack about his
mother made Lou see red. He charged across the
diamond as the team changed at the end of an inning
and, first up, went for Cobb. Ty, not wishing to

tangle with this human locomotive, stepped nimbly out of the way, and Lou, continuing his bull-like charge, ran head-on into the roof of the dugout.

Detroit players picked him up and held him while he shook his head clear and then assisted him back to the Yankee bench. After the game the two would-be battlers shook hands. Cobb seemed relieved that he hadn't been forced to fight Lou and was willing to call it quits. As a matter of record, afterward, he was a great admirer of Gehrig's and occasionally advised him on finer points of the game. Finally, he chose Lou on his all-star, all-time team.

Gehrig's social relationships improved with his ball game. Under the kindly wing of the Babe, Lou was introduced to the intricacies of bridge. After some strenuous preliminary coaching, he sat down to the first game of his life. The rest around the table were just as anxious to make it easy on Lou (ballplayers never played for fun) as Lou was anxious to show that he was a good sport.

'One cent a point?' suggested one.

'Don't make it as low as that,' said Lou quickly. The stake was fixed at five cents a point. On the second hand Lou bid and, of course, went down three hundred points.

'That'll cost you fifteen dollars,' the Babe observed.

'My!' said the surprised Gehrig. 'This is certainly a game for sharpies!' and he began to settle down to business.

He studied bridge faithfully for a year, and became, finally, the best player on the Yankee team.

As Lou's chunky figure became a fixture around the Yankee first sack, he became increasingly famous. He was invited in 1925, just after the season closed, to join in a stunt tournament. He was to compete with Leo Diegel, who had been Canadian open golf champion for the past two years, Paul Crouch, who was the champion archer of the United States, and Edwin Harkins, the champion rod-and-line man of the United States, over nine holes of golf. Diegel would play as usual, Lou would bat or throw a baseball, Crouch would shoot arrows (ending with a target on the green), and Harkins would cast a fly.

Lou won the bizarre publicity affair by finishing one stroke less than Diegel, who made it in 33, three under par. Twelve hundred spectators watched the tournament. But they seemed to be more impressed with Harkins's feat of casting a fly than they seemed to be with Lou's really gargantuan tosses and fungoes.

'This is a crazy business,' Lou said afterward, 'but it's a living.' He got two hundred and fifty dollars for the afternoon. When the stunt was repeated in 1927, Lou came in a bad second to Crouch.

In these days none of the sports writers or baseball men outside those on the big-league teams seemed to know quite what to make of this chunk of muscle from Morningside Heights. He seemed too well bred and quiet and affable to make a really good ballplayer. His very genuine clumsiness around the premier sack seemed to bear this opinion out, as well as his unabashed attachment to his mother and general diffidence to the usual ballplayer ways.

But his hitting put him in a different light.

'It is a fearsome thing to see him — shaking his clenched fist at the pitcher, grabbing grounders in his great hands, swinging for the fences, pawing at the rubber with his spikes,' wrote one sports observer.

No one could foresee the future, least of all Lou. No one could know what was coming up in the next two years, how this indestructible would strike at the home of the gods within two years, the Valhalla where the great Babe Ruth had dwelt alone for so many years.

Gehrig was set with the Yankees. And with Gehrig and the Babe the Yankees were set for the most glorious years in the history of America's national game. A new era of prosperity, a boom in good living was already on its way, a typically rabelaisian and American era of which Ruth was to be the symbol of the high-wide-and-handsome and Gehrig the symbol of the steadier, saner values of the nation.

By 1926 destiny was shaping the rough-hewn end of Lou. The Columbia colossus was willing to follow where it led — as long as he could take Christina and

Heinrich Gehrig along. The three of them moved into a new four-room apartment in Morningside Heights, just across from the Park.

The neighborhood kids used to play in the Park eternally at pick-up baseball, and the legend was that when Lou drove home from the Yankee Stadium in his second-hand Chevrolet, he would rush into the apartment, kiss Christina, and rush out again, shirt-sleeved and hatless, to play with the kids.

Lou was a hero of sorts now, to more than a flock of school-kids. He was already touted as the man to dethrone the Sultan of Swat and many felt that Ruth's head must be uneasy, wearing so precarious a crown. When the spring of 1926 rolled around, Lou packed up and went off to the training ground of the Yankees in St. Petersburg, Florida. He was happier than he had ever been in his life. He was ready to make come true what half of the ball fans in New York and the country believed he could do and what the other half suspected he could do.

With him went Christina, to sit placidly on the porch of a St. Petersburg hotel, dreaming in the sun and waiting for Louie to come home so that she could cook his supper after the day's workout. It became a tradition for Lou's mother to accompany him for six weeks' vacation on the training-camp trips.

Lou used to have his first really good times in base-ball, running happily around the track with three sweatshirts on, his surplus poundage running off his crash-chassis in rivulets; taking his showers and loosening up his muscles under the eyes of the ever-and-omnipresent gaffer baseball nuts of the town; bicycling on his back; looking into the black boxes that had once scared him for the photographers; hitting, pitching, fielding in all the thousand-and-one training looseners that Huggins thought up for his crew of baseball behemoths.

There was always one drawback to St. Petersburg for Lou, however. In all his seven years of training there, Lou never managed to hit but one home run. The mighty Babe would boom them out, one after the other, to the screaming edification of the stands, but Lou found that all his stick-work invariably came later.

Going into the 1926 season Lou already had a reputation to sustain. He had made something of a name for himself as a pinch-hitter in ten games of 1924. The newspapers had played him up, and Huggins always expected his players to make suckers of newspaper clippings.

As a matter of fact, Lou had something of a hex on American League pitchers. He had not been around long enough for them to get a good background of dope on him. He had blasted the legend that he could not hit fast balls by simply murdering each one as it came up to the plate. Lou was an absolutely fearless hitter and stepped into each swing with a vigor only surpassed by the Babe.

Nor did the opposing pitchers have much hope that Lou would have the inexplainable slumps of the Babe.

'He'll never slump, he's too strong,' they said. 'Did you ever see a bull slump?'

For some time they had entertained hope that they could pitch low and outside to Lou and keep the outfield edging over to left and center. For a time Lou had hit consistently to those pastures. But the Babe's coaching on how to pull hits into right cured that. The pitchers still remembered how laboriously the southpaw Rube Walberg had worked on Gehrig one day in late 1925, finally ending up with a slow curve, low and outside, pitched with infinite care to the exact spot where Rube wanted it to go.

As the ball hooked up to the plate, Lou lashed out. He smashed the ball onto the right-field bleachers for a home run. The same thing happened to Lefty Grove — and it made no difference whether the park was the huge Yankee Stadium or the confines of Shibe Park in Philadelphia. Lou seemed to pickle them all.

The pitchers knew that Babe would do one of three things — walk, strike out, or homer. But they felt that Lou was liable to hit anything, anywhere, at any given time. Now, worst of all, they would have to pitch to the Babe. Huggins had announced that Lou would precede the Babe in the batting order, much to the latter's joy. They couldn't afford to pass two men, and the Babe, who had offered to hit the ball right-handed, with one hand, or even standing on his head if only the pitchers would stop giving him deliberate walks, felt fine about the Yanks' new recruit. In many ways, indeed, it was spotting Lou just ahead of Ruth that way that made the Babe break his own record of fifty-nine home runs in 1927 — and that kept Lou forever just a pace behind the Bambino in home-run hitting.

Lou was still in great awe of the Babe — as he was to remain until the end of his baseball days. He had a whole flock of anecdotes about the great one's idiosyncrasies. He told John Kieran of the *New York Times*:

> The Babe was the biggest man in the world to me. I was goggle-eyed just from looking at him — from a distance. I was too timid to go near him. Well, one day he went out to the races and won about four thousand dollars. He carried his winnings in four bills in his pocket. He took a taxi back to the hotel and gave the driver a bill and told him to keep the change. He thought it was a dollar bill. But it was a thousand-dollar bill and the driver kept the change. The Babe didn't find out until later and he never did see the driver again.

The Babe roared about that mistake, but what made him loom so large in Lou's eyes was the fact that he didn't really care too much. Lou would have been despondent for days over such an error. Both boys had beeen raised in pinched circumstances. But Babe Ruth had come out of it with a roaring forties complex of money-scattering, while Lou had learned the frugal German ways of saving for the future.

He rarely bought any new clothes, even though he was now getting eight thousand dollars a year and had all the money he needed. He cut a sober figure among the fine feathers of his team-mates, who insisted on twenty-dollar silk shirts and Charvet ties and twenty-five dollar shoes of kangaroo leather to play in.

'I felt like a tramp,' Lou used to say with a laugh. He never took a taxi to the ball park — he always used a trolley or walked.

But Lou seemed not to feel the need of the usual citizen's clothing or transportation. There is the story of the winter's day when snow was swirling about the windows of the Yankee office and the bitter cold was striking into the steam-heated room right through the frost-rimmed windows. Over the radiator were huddled a few frost-bitten Yankee players.

The door slammed open and in strode the man who was known as Lou, full of fire and zing, blood flushing his cheeks, without hat or overcoat — or even coat. As a concession to the seasonal weather, Lou did have his shirtsleeves down.

Some chilled wight spoke up: 'Where's your coat, Lou?'

'Never bother with them!' cried the exuberant Lou. 'They get in my way! Boy, what fine weather!' He departed in a gust of snowflakes and left the Yankees staring after him.

'Look at him,' one murmured. 'That guy is as hard as rocks!'

Lou never let himself down. He kept his condition one year after another. His weight bothered him at first but he got it down to around two hundred and ten, and after that kept an eye on it so that in the off-months of the year he would usually only gain a pound or so. His main worry was about his legs. He still remembered Cobb's scornful comment.

'I try to keep the leg muscles limber,' he said. 'I stretch 'em every day for about five minutes. I think I'm good enough as far as the other muscles are concerned But they say the legs go first, and I'm taking care of mine.'

Yet Lou knew as well as anyone that in these first years of his regular big-league job his chief worry was not his condition, nor his hitting, nor his speed (he was quite fast for a big fellow). His main drawback was his slow mind, not yet attuned to the automatic reflexes of baseball, tending to become confused in an emergency — plus his clumsy body co-ordination.

So he began a siege of training for himself at the Stadium. Each day he would show up at noon, hours before the game, and start his own personal fielding

practice. He would get Coach Charlie O'Leary to hit
grounders and flies to him, ball after ball.

Lou discovered that he was bad on ground balls.
They got by him before he could get his hands ready
for them. He didn't use his hands and arms right
somehow. He didn't get the throws he should have.
He was weak on his left side.

His arms hung down too close in, like a gorilla's.
The hands seemed to hang wrong on the ends of his
wrist, turned in too much, too straight down, too
close to his legs. They weren't far enough out for Lou
to get free and loose play with them. Actually they
reflected his self-consciousness.

Huggins had told Lou that in so many words. He
had added that he would benefit if he would loosen up
with arms and hands, wave them, swing them out
wider, let them flop relaxed and range without stiff-
ness.

Lou caught the general idea. He practiced before
games every year until 1929. And at that time Huggins viewed a finished product.

'Lou increased his catching range by five feet,'
said Huggins proudly. Lou, hearing it, grinned. 'I
was sure a bum fielder,' he said, recalling the days in
1926 when he started. 'Maybe I am now, but I'm a
lot better than I was.'

About his hitting there was never any question.
The race with the Babe began with the season, and

for a time the two giants of Murderer's Row, Larrupin' Lou and the King of Swat, were batting them
over the fence in almost perfect unison.

The first home run Lou hit was a line drive to left
that went directly into the bleachers. As Lou rounded
third and came into home standing up the Babe was
waiting for him.

'Nice goin', kid,' said the Babe, trotting to the
dugout with him. 'But remember it's a long way to
the record. I found that out.'

The accolade that Lou always appreciated the
most came in 1926 in a game with Cleveland. At the
time — in the late spring — Lou and the Babe were
running neck-and-neck in the home-run race, nine
to nine. Lou had just tied the Babe in that same
game and the next time he came up to bat, the great
park was silent.

Lou knocked the dirt from his spikes, pulled down
his cap, and waited. The ball came up and Lou
fouled it. Two balls were called and Lou took a clean
cut and missed. There was a sigh from the stands.
On the fifth ball, the pellet hooked across the outside
corner of the plate and Lou let it go by.

'Strike three!' shouted the umpire and brought
down his arm.

The crowd broke out into a roar of joy. To Lou,
going back to the dugout, that medley of cheers and
boos — mostly boos — was music, for it meant that

for the first time fandom as well as the men in baseball accepted him as a first-rate batting menace. To
be that on the Yankee team, next to the Babe in the
lineup, was honor indeed in those days.

Gehrig's fame was cropping out in other ways, too.
One day he came up to the Yankee Stadium on his
way to a game with St. Louis and found a gang of men
blocking the players' gate. A single policeman was
holding back with an upraised arm a mob of about
twenty-five clamoring men.

'What's the trouble?' Lou inquired.

'It's these guys, Lou, wanting to crash the game,'
said the bluecoat. 'This big lug here says he's Rogers
Hornsby and the rest say they're the St. Louis team,
but they can't produce anything to prove it.'

Lou looked around. He looked full into the irate
gaze of the great Hornsby. He turned back to the
cop.

'Let 'em in, Joe,' he said hastily. 'They're telling
the truth.'

'Thanks,' growled Rogers sarcastically as he went
by.

Lou made only sixteen home runs in 1926, in spite
of the fact that early in the season he was making a
brave bid for Ruth's laurels. The trouble was that he
was still learning — and still had much to learn. The
fact that he led the league in triples — twenty of
them — indicates the power of his hitting much bet-

ter. Lou *was* hitting, and well, too. But he had not learned, as yet, to pull his hits to places where they would result in the most extra bases.

Knowing this himself, Lou took to studying a new base hit — a short, chopped hit into left as well as a pulled right ball. He stayed in every game, not thinking of any record, simply to study and study the way he had once kept his nose in schoolbooks.

There were times when staying in the game was a tough proposition. Once a hard-hit grounder took an unscheduled hop and smacked Lou squarely on the nose. It didn't break the bone, luckily, but the impact blackened both eyes. Lou kept right on playing, that day and the next day, with those purple, swollen eyes.

At another time he was suffering from a fever, but he took no notice of it. Instead, he played his regular position and proved that he was far from a handicap to his team-mates by hitting three triples the day that his temperature was at its height.

Lou had an obsession about not being X-rayed. Not even after an injury on the field would he allow himself to go under the ray — preferring to remain a player on the old Spartan school who took his bruises and wounds in silence.

'The doctors would probably discover that I have broken a thumb or a finger or chipped a bone in my foot, which would mean I would have to lay off,' said

Lou. 'I would prefer not to know the extent of my injuries and keep on playing.'

Doctors, amazed at his physical endurance, often examined Lou to find out the secret of the Iron Horse. But the most they could make out of this most durable of baseball's men-at-arms was the fact that the electro-cardiograph showed that Lou had an extremely small heart. This, they said, indicated that Lou's heart would return to normal in about seventy-two seconds, even with maximum effort, in a ball game. A big pump that had to shoot Lou's two hundred and ten pounds around the bases in record time might take two or three hours to calm down, but his small heart, like that of Clarence De Mar, the dean of marathoners, and Paavo Nurmi, the long-distance running Finn, could take it easily.

Adding that fact to his unusually powerful physique and his acquired baseball sense, the medical fraternity decided that Gehrig was one of the world's finest physical specimens when it came to playing ball.

Lou never developed that split-second thinking that is more of a physical reflex than an actual thought. Most ball players have it naturally. It tells them what to do without thinking. The Babe, for example, never threw to a wrong base in his life, and often broke up a game by starting with the crack of the ball on the bat and scooping up a would-be hit from his shoe tops. Somehow he knew just where every ball should be thrown, where every ball should be fielded.

Lou had to teach himself all these departments — except his hitting, where he was completely natural. He had a characteristic pose at the plate that soon gave him the name of 'biscuit-pants.' It was a humped position, feet well apart, bending over the plate with his eyes fastened on the pitcher. Lou never indulged in batting histrionics. He merely waggled the tip of his bat a fraction of an inch as he waited, then stepped forward into the ball. He rarely struck at bad balls.

On the bases, he never achieved prominence. His idea of running bases was to pay strict attention to the coach, then, head down, to run as fast and hard as he could to the next base. He could never do the star base-running of his twin home-run hitter, the Babe. Once in a 1928 World Series, the Babe discombobulated the whole audience and players in a game by stealing third and home with a lame knee.

Lou, however, had his own special qualities that endeared him to managers and players — reliability and non-temperament, coupled with top-notch playing ability. He was ready now for 1927, one of his finest seasons.

Larrupin' Lou

In 1927 the most frequently used regulars of the Yankee team were these: Benny Bengough, Bob Meusel, Tony Lazzeri, Joe Dugan, Mark Koenig, Earl Combs — and, of course, Babe Ruth and Lou Gehrig. The pitchers were Waite Hoyt, Herb Pennock, Urban Shocker, and young Wilcy Moore.

That was the famous lineup that swept the Yanks to their fame back in the ball-mad days of 1927. Murderers' Row — which was always an indefinite term which no one ever fully delineated, like the line between the eastern and western hemispheres — was usually composed of five hitters. These sluggers were Combs, Lazzeri, Meusel — and, of course, Babe Ruth and Lou Gehrig.

The two murderous twins, Babe and Lou, were just beginning to be known as twins. The Babe, who had been with the Yanks for seven years, and who had

broken into his first World Series in 1921, had ruled
the hitting-roost of the Yanks for so long that no one
seriously believed anyone could ever come up to
challenge him.

Yet that was what Lou Gehrig bade fair to do. He
already held one crown which had for a long time been
the Babe's specialty — runs batted in. He was such a
power at the bat that, according to Manager Miller
Huggins's estimate of him, he was soon put in fourth
position, just after Ruth.

The Babe never seemed to resent Lou's displacing
him in the clean-up spot. He knew he had his audience forever in the palm of his hand and that no new-
comer, least of all one as unspectacular and unassuming as Lou, would replace him in their boisterous
affections. He was the first to recognize Lou's talents
and made the famous compact with him that they
would work as team-mates, not as spotlight rivals.

'That's one for us,' was the motto of this duo, repeated as a sporting litany after either of them had
smashed a long hit.

That year, when good cheer and fun were flowing
freely across the United States, when workingmen
bought silk shirts and chorus girls were still given
diamonds and sables by more than one man a week,
when hundred-dollar tips to waiters were not uncom-
mon, and Katharine Brush and Scott Fitzgerald
indulged in their rhapsodic melancholia over their

lost generation, the Yanks had as good a year as anyone.

They won the American League pennant — not by a spectacular lead, but by a good margin. Most of all, they had developed the full-blown reputation of being the most devastating hitting aggregation of all time in baseball.

When Miller Huggins had come to the Yankees in 1917, his first two seasons had resulted in third-place teams. This was undoubtedly due to arguments with the temperamental, hot-dog-eating, pop-drinking Babe and trying to keep the vociferous Lippy Leo Durocher — now manager of the Brooklyn team in the National League — in the lineup. The Babe was Hug's personal problem. He simply disobeyed orders on and off the field until Hug fined him five thousand dollars in 1925, was backed up by both Colonel Ruppert and Ed Barrow, and the Babe quieted down into just being a ballplayer instead of a clown. But Leo was a rambunctious, acid-tongued player, albeit one of the best short-stops in the game. His team-mates made no secret of the fact that they didn't like him and eventually Hug, in spite of his admiration for Durocher's skill at short-stop, had to trade him off.

For the next three years, the Yankees won the league pennant as Hug resolutely kept squabbles between himself and Ruth and between Durocher and the rest of the team down to a minimum. In 1921 and

1922, the Yankees were trounced in the World Series.

Their first world's championship came in 1923, the year that Lou Gehrig had first visited the clubhouse to see and hero-worship.

Both 1924 and 1925 were sub-standard seasons for the Yankees. Although they won second place in 1924, New York had come to expect nothing but champions. In 1925 they sank to seventh. Huggins was busy ironing out his team difficulties for good and rebuilding both men and morale. Lou Gehrig was coming up, possibly as a successor to Ruth, possibly as an addition to Murderers' Row.

In 1926 the league pennant went to the Yankees, but the St. Louis Cardinals, in a neck-and-neck series, beat them out for the championship of both leagues.

But the next two years the Yankees set a record. They smashed through to win the American League pennants by top-heavy margins and then went on to win both World Series in eight straight games — a devastating display of the power that Miller Huggins had been building up.

The Babe, by the time the 1927 season had closed, had reaped the full reward of all his years in baseball. He had reached the pinnacle of sixty home runs. He was one of the major idols of the country, in a time when idols were plentiful — among them being a young man named Charles Lindbergh who flew the Atlantic solo in thirty-three hours.

In all the sound and fury of those days, Lou remained as he had been. He was big, good-natured, powerful, the perfect embodiment of everything that all expected of him. He was getting eight thousand dollars a year, had a few new suits, could buy Christina any number of things that she didn't want but which he wanted to give her, and was perfectly happy.

He kept his sense of values amazingly well. In days when money was rushing past him in torrents, going around with the free-spending Babe, who once lost two hundred thousand dollars in one winter season at Havana, seeing his team-mates in two-hundred-dollar suits and silk socks and underwear, Lou kept his money and put it away in bonds and savings.

But he never had — or wanted — the ability to comprehend high finance the way his friend Babe did. At the end of 1927, the first year he displayed all the gigantic promise that later made him an unanimous choice of virtually all baseball critics for one of the five all-time baseball greats, the Babe called him aside.

'Lou,' he said in a kindly tone, 'I want to give you a tip.'

Lou listened attentively.

'You remember when you came to me the other day and asked me what you should get for 1928?'

Lou nodded.

'Well,' the Babe went on, 'I've thought it over and

I say you shouldn't get a cent less than thirty thousand dollars.'

Lou's eyes bulged. The previous season he had received exactly eight thousand dollars. His head whirled as he figured up the amount, and all he could think of was what to do with the money. His own tastes were simple. He had gone to the Yankee training camp in New Orleans in 1924 with only a ten-dollar bill in his pocket, picking up extra cash by dishwashing on the side. The only thing he could think of was to buy presents for Christina.

'Not a cent less than thirty thousand dollars,' repeated the Babe portentously. 'I know what I'm talking about. Promise me you won't take less. I know what you're worth.'

Lou promised and nothing more was said. Lou went into the salary negotiations, came out in record time, his face beaming, and Ruth assumed that all was well.

But a few days later, the Babe picked up a local newspaper. On the front page was spread the news that Lou had signed a two-year contract for twenty-five thousand dollars a year.

The Babe stormed around and finally located Lou practicing on the field.

'What's this?' demanded the Babe, apoplectic-red. 'I thought I told you to hold out for thirty grand. You would have got it, too. I know. And I thought you promised me.'

A look of surprise came over Lou's face.

'But, Babe,' he protested, 'I'm going to get more. I didn't break my promise. Look, I got a contract for fifty thousand dollars not thirty thousand.'

Sometimes his thrifty ways didn't make him feel too comfortable in the company of the high-living Yankees, but for the life of him he could not forget his frugal childhood and the habits that Christina had taught him. He always got up early, went to the ball park and did a little practicing with one of the coaches. After the game, he would dress hurriedly and rush out to go home and get 'my mom's home cooking.'

To the point where it would have been ridiculous if it had not been so sincere, Lou was the personification of all the virtues that mothers point out to their boys as ideal. Yet he was all that unconsciously, bobbing his curly brown head and grinning bashfully as he talked in slow accents to reporters, giving them his idea of life and how to live it.

Lou was always careful about 'the kids.' If he was being photographed, he always made sure that his favorite briar pipe was out of his mouth. 'It would give the kids bad ideas,' he explained once at an interview. 'I don't want it said that I was the one to start some youngster smoking.'

His first thought when he began getting a good salary from the Yankees was for his mother Christina and Heinrich. He bought them a little white house on Meadowlane, New Rochelle, and treated it like a baby himself. Days off from baseball, any reporter could find Lou Gehrig with a paint-stained cap on and smeared overalls painting or puttying around the house. The visor of the cap would be turned toward the rear and the sleeves of his work shirt rolled up. He would give an interview as he worked.

'I saw this house in September, 1927,' he said to one reporter. 'I fell in love with it right then. It was my kind of a house. Look at those trees, real big ones, real forest trees. They're bigger even than the ones you see in Central Park. It's got eight or nine rooms, three floors, and a basement. I tell you it's just what I've always wanted.'

Even in the chill of January, he still tinkered around the house, making odd repairs.

'I'm not going to spend a cent of my new salary,' Lou said to his friends. 'I'm going to salt it all away, and mom and me will live on what I get on the side for endorsements and things.'

He gave the deed to the house to his parents for a Christmas present, putting it under the Christmas tree in imitation of a Christmas long ago when he had got his first baseball mitt. Then he repaired the house and had a sleeping porch put on.

'Breathe in some of that air out here,' he said proudly.

'Can that stuff about marriage,' Lou said in 1927 and 1928. 'I'm all right just as I am. Don't run around writing any of that stuff. I'll never marry as long as my mom is living.'

Lou would point with pride to Christina, who would be rocking on the porch and beaming.

'She's only forty-six now, so you guys can make up your minds how much chance I want to marry,' he said. 'Leave me alone. I'm embarrassed enough as it is with a girls' school just up the street.'

Lou used to boast how he saved money on odds and ends. 'I never wear an overcoat or a vest,' he boasted. 'There's something saved right there.'

He set his father up in the ornamental-iron mechanic trade again when he had fully recovered from his illness. For Christina he brought the eels he caught in Long Island Sound.

The year of 1927 had marked the first time that Babe Ruth and Lou Gehrig came into violent contact — spiritually speaking. For the first time in the juggernaut career of the Babe, his home-run record was threatened. But there was never any indication of anything but the friendliest rivalry. Each player rooted for the other.

Once when Ruth had housemaid's knee and had to stay off the field as an active player, he hobbled up and down the coaching box, yelling hoarse encouragement to Gehrig — who, like as not, would line-

drive a long hit and churn down the base paths past
the Babe on his way home.

That year saw a ding-dong battle in the matter of
home runs. On June 30, the twins were tied with
24 each.

'The only man who will ever beat my record,' said
the Babe proudly, 'is old Larrupin' Lou.'

On July 27 they were tied again, 33 to 33. July 31,
Lou was ahead, 35 to 34. Then on August 17 they
were tied again, 38 to 38. On August 25 they were
knotted at 40 to 40.

On September 6 at Fenway Park, Boston, Lou hit
his forty-fifth home run in the fifth inning, putting
him one up on the Babe. Then the Babe, in the sixth
inning, swung from his heels and drove one into the
center-field bleachers to tie it up again.

From then on there was no staying Ruth. He had
smelled the smoke of battle, and in the seventh he
drove another into the right-field bleachers, in the
ninth a third into the same place. He was ahead,
47 to 45, and Lou could never head him.

The next day Babe hit two more — but Lou got
none.

They ended the season with the Babe making a new
record of sixty home runs and Lou getting forty-
seven. Their breath-taking contest in long-range
hitting had made them the most popular two men
in the country.

It was announced that they would make an exhibition tour of the country, playing in fifteen games. It stretched into twenty-one games and the most extraordinary tour in the history of baseball.

They played in twenty cities from Rhode Island to California and in nine different states. They traveled eight thousand miles and were seen by two hundred and twenty thousand people, autographed five thousand balls.

Thirteen of the twenty-one games were never finished. The enthusiastic fans broke down all barriers, swarmed on the field, and swept their heroes away. Both Babe and Lou pitched, fielded, played the infield — but most of all they were hitting.

In one game at Asbury Park, New Jersey, they knocked thirty-five balls over the fence. Babe pitched the thirty-sixth one to Lou and Gehrig sent it sailing over the fence into a lagoon. The game was over — the management had only thought to bring three dozen balls.

Lou was his usual effacing self. But the Babe stole the show. He hit nearly every time on the first ball pitched, nearly always for a home run. He ran the bases with a fountain-pen in his pocket, signing balls and tokens at every base. He once held up a game for an hour and a half, waiting to get a certified check for twenty-five hundred dollars.

That triumphal tour broke all records. It ended up with the following averages:

	At Bat	Hits	Home Runs	Percentage
Gehrig......	89	55	13	.618
Ruth........	99	61	20	.616

Be it noted that the Babe got the most home runs and hits — as well as the most times at bat — but that Lou out-hit him in percentages.

Neither Lou nor the Babe ever revealed how much they made from the trip, but it was well up in five figures for both of them.

That tour gave a halo to Lou's record for the bonanza year of 1927. Lou, during the playing season, smashed out 218 hits for 447 bases; he made 47 home runs, 18 triples, and 52 doubles. He made a new record by driving in 175 runs.

During 1928, the rivalry of the home-run twins was renewed. Lou, on his first twenty-five thousand dollars of his two-year contract, was impossible to down. Early in the season he distinguished himself at fielding — a feat that made the phlegmatic Huggins get up off the bench to congratulate him. He completed two double plays unassisted against the Chicago White Sox. Six days later, he proved himself to be still the redoubtable siege-gun of the preceding season. Lou walloped two triples and two home runs in four trips to the plate. June 26, the Yankees performed their famous feat of smashing eleven runs over the plate in the twelfth inning to coast to victory.

By this time Lou was no longer being pitched to. He was feared as much as the Babe. Together, they gave opposing pitchers the shivers — knowing that both Lou, with his peculiar bent-over stance, that slight wiggle of his bat, and the Babe, with his upright, spindly power-posture, would be ready to lash into the ball.

Between the two of them, they supplied the punch to give Miller Huggins his sixth pennant — the second string of three straight for the diminutive manager.

In the World Series of 1928, young Lou further distinguished himself. The six-foot-one slugger came out with top home-run honors in the series — driving four of the nine credited to the Yanks. This ran him neck and neck with the Babe, who had accomplished precisely the same feat in 1926.

Lou also batted in nine runs and was instrumental in the Yanks' scoring a victory over the Cardinal crew in four straight games. He got two home runs in the third game after getting one in the second. In the final game, Babe and Lou hit successive home runs in the seventh inning. The Cardinal pitchers handed Lou five bases in balls in two games.

In 1929, several events occurred which were to affect the course of Lou's life deeply. That year was a comparatively poor season for the Yanks. They fell to second place in the league after being invincible for three years.

Lou himself slumped to an average of an even .300 — an average that many batsmen would give their eye-teeth to achieve, but a notable slump for the slugging Lou. He did his thirty-five home runs — eight more than he had hit the year before — and his fielding had improved to its peak. He had also hit three home runs in a single game on May 4, for the second time in his career.

But all these things did not make up, either for Lou or for the public, for the things that this superman of swat was supposed to do. Everybody, all around, felt let down.

On top of that, in September, 1929, Miller Huggins died. He had been the best manager that the Yankees ever had up to that time. The fans of New York, however, had not liked him any too well. Babe Ruth, when he came to the Yanks, had acted pretty much as he pleased and Huggins had been forced to crack down on the Bambino for his disobedience to orders. This had brought matters to a head before Colonel Ruppert, and Huggins had been upheld.

This did not increase Huggins's popularity with either the fans or the players. Once a disgruntled Yankee, according to the story, who had been drinking too much, grabbed Huggins while the team was en route to its next game. The player, who was an outsize Man Mountain Dean, took Hug back to the observation car and dangled the manager just above the flickering ties. Huggins never uttered a cry and was placed back on the platform. The player was released.

Leo Durocher, as has been said, was, as ever, the other Huggins problem. Hug liked him, thought him a fine short-stop, but Lippy could not get along with the team or the fans and was finally released.

But slowly the Yankees built up and Huggins began to win pennants and world-championship titles. New York grew to adore him, and in the flush days of 1928 he was a baseball hero.

In those days this incident was only a joke. Lou had been on base and had been slow getting back. The umpire had called him out. Lou complained — loud and bitterly. But not too bitterly, as Lou was very careful about being fined.

Huggins heard the uproar and came darting out on the field. The umpire, who had had just about enough from Lou at that point, saw Huggins coming over.

'You,' he roared, pointing to Lou. 'You take yourself off this field. And —' pointing dramatically to Manager Huggins — 'take that bat boy with you.'

Hug's death was a tragedy. Blood poisoning came upon him and ravaged his system. Blood transfusions from the team were tried in an attempt to save his life, but they were useless.

Crowds fought to get into the Church Around the Corner, off Fifth Avenue in New York, to see the dead manager. And among the crowd was Lou Gehrig, serious, cap in hand. When he walked past the open coffin and saw the pale face of Hug, Lou wept. Ever after that he had a horror of funerals, a horror that was to make his own one of the most inconspicuous in the history of baseball.

That same year, after the season had closed, Lou announced that he had become associated with a brokerage firm. It was just after the crash, when everyone was still hoping that the tumbling stock prices were just temporary.

The firm was Appenfellar, Allen and Hill, on Wall Street, and Lou said that he had decided to take a desk there. He pointed out that a ballplayer couldn't last forever — though he intended playing as long as he could — and that it wasn't a good policy to put too many eggs in a single basket.

The terms and the windup of that association have never been published. Lou left the firm soon after. It was never known how much or if any losses were sustained by him.

In 1930, both 'Jidge' — as the Yankees called Ruth — and 'Slug' — as they called Lou — opened up the season of home runs officially — Lou on April 19, the Babe on April 26. Each clouted one. It was an auspicious beginning for Lou, and he lived up to it.

By the end of the 1930 season he had hit for a high of .379, his highest batting average in his baseball career. He got back the runs-battled-in title which he had left by default in 1929 and held it for the next two seasons. Forty-one home runs rattled off his bat.

On May 21, 1930, Babe Ruth hit three successive home runs against the Athletics. May 22, Lou duplicated the feat. Lou continued his way by smashing out a double, triple, and two homers later in the season, indicating that his renewed zest for lambasting was hardly a flash in the pan.

Part of Lou's success in hitting in 1930 was due to the fact that the Yankees, under the direction of Bob Shawkey, were running neck and neck for a long time with the Cleveland Indians. Roger Peckinpaugh, manager of the Indians, was determined to take no chances with Babe Ruth. He wanted no games broken up by home runs. He instructed his pitchers to pass Ruth and pitch to Lou.

It was a mistake. In the eleven games against the Indians, Lou made twenty-four hits in forty-six times at bat — an average of .522. In one three-game series in Cleveland, Lou made sixteen runs across the plate for an American League record.

About the middle of the season, John McGraw, canny and famous pilot of the New York Giants, was asked to name a mythical all-star team for all time. McGraw named Lou over Bill Terry, his own star first-sacker.

During these days Lou was playing with such vim

that half the time his thighs were swathed in bandages from his cannon-like sliding into bases. He had no thought for himself, and went all out on every possible play that came anywhere near his jurisdiction.

Lou disregarded an injured finger that was broken three weeks before the end of the season, but after it had closed he had operations both on his elbow, which was splintered, and a cyst in his right ear at St. Vincent's Hospital in New York.

Although he trailed Ruth in home runs again, there was no malice — nor even as much rivalry as the crowds would have liked. When Babe decided to open up a haberdashery shop in New York, Lou was on hand to help him dedicate it. He tried on various sizes of hats under the sweltering Klieg lights of the motion-picture cameras, made wisecracks, and posed with his arms around Babe's neck.

The next year was another outstanding one for Lou. Joe McCarthy had replaced Bob Shawkey as manager. Joe was new to the American League and the Yankees, but he had done a creditable job for Chicago in the National. He took the Yanks, who had finished third in 1930, and pushed them up one notch to second.

The touch-and-go part of that season was the home-run race again. For a long time it had threatened to be a close thing, but always, at the last moment, the Babe had run off with it. This year Lou did not let him get out of his sight.

At the end of the season, each had forty-six.

By all odds, Lou should have had the home-run championship that year. It would have pleased him more than anything else and by rights it was his. Yet a peculiar incident had robbed him of it.

In April, Lou had smacked a long, screaming drive out to the right-field barrier. Lyn Lary was on base. Lou, seeing that the ball was a sure home run, nevertheless refused to slacken pace and pounded on. Lary, however, thinking it had been caught, turned off at third and went to the dugout. Lou, as will be related in detail later, passed the spot where Lary had been and was automatically out.

It was Joe McCarthy who made the immortal remark on that incident afterward. He gathered the players around — Lou was glaring at Lary, since if there was anything that both he and the Babe took seriously it was home-run hitting — and addressed them:

'Gentlemen,' he said gently, 'Lyn didn't know that Lou had hit a home run.' His voice sharpened. 'Hereafter, we will devise a set of signals so that everyone will know that a certain ball is tagged for a home run.' His voice became acidulous. 'I want no secrets on this team.'

As it was, Lou went on hitting them, one for one with the Babe, until the last game of the season at the Stadium, where he was one home run behind. There, before a crowd of forty thousand, he smashed the final home run that brought him into the record book on even terms at last with the Babe.

Various people selected Lou as the most valuable player in the American League that year. He had put on one of his classic exhibitions of hitting — six home runs in six successive games, a new league record of one hundred and eighty-four runs batted in, a batting average of .341.

That year too, both the Babe and Lou demonstrated that chivalry, at least in baseball, is not dead. In an exhibition game in Chattanooga, Tennessee, Jackie Mitchell, touted to be the only girl pitcher in baseball, was put up against the mighty twins of swat.

Babe got up first, hefting his bat and grinning at the nervous girl in the box. With abandon worthy of a Barrymore, he took three mighty whiffs. Then Lou came up to the cheers of the crackers, grinning from ear to ear. With methodical preciseness, Lou also took three wide swings, and the day was a success with all concerned.

One thing is worth noting that happened in 1931 which never happened again. In a regular game that May, McCarthy used Babe Ruth on first and Lou in right field. The switch came about because of the Babe's bad leg.

Just after the finish of the World Series — in which the Yanks failed to participate — a group of players went to Japan to tour in exhibition games. The Babe and Lou Gehrig went along.

The aggregation played seventeen games and won all of them. As usual, the Japanese, from the Mikado down to the fishermen, were enthusiastic about the American pastime. Over half a million slant-eyed fans jammed the parks of the various cities, notably in Tokyo, where in four games there was an average of fifty-five thousand in attendance.

Lou was the hero of the Japanese. But it cost him a broken hand. Once, before a game, he consented to give a short lecture on baseball to a group of Japanese players. He talked to them solemnly and slowly for a time until a small, shaven-headed Japanese pushed his way to the front of the crowd.

'Please, Mr. Lou,' he squeaked, 'if the honorable batter were very good and very fearless and crowded the honorable plate, what would humble person pitcher be expected to do?'

Lou gave him an immediate answer. 'I should say a dusting off was in order,' he said. He proceeded to explain that 'dusting off' meant sending a ball at the head of the batter to make him move back.

That afternoon Lou stepped up to the plate to take his cut and peered at the pitcher. To his amazement, the little Japanese looked familiar. It was the same man who had asked the question. Lou tightened his grip.

The pitch came. It was a straight, hard, fast ball. It flew directly at Lou. Lou flung up his hands and ducked. The ball caught him on his right hand and broke two bones.

During this trip Lou spent most of his time buying presents for Christina — they finally totalled eight hundred dollars. He saw an Oriental wrestling match which he described as 'a couple of specially bred five hundred-pound human hippos trying to shove one another outside a ten-foot ring.'

Lou went on a similar trip in 1934. Asked his impressions of this as an old Japanese hand, Lou said that he had a grand time playing to whooping crowds and that besides the twenty-two Japanese games they had played one in Honolulu, one in Shanghai, and three in Manila.

'I played left field most of the time,' he said. 'Ruth was on first. Our club made at least fifty homers on the tour, the Big Fellow getting about twelve or fourteen. I guess I made about ten.

'We played with both American and Japanese-made baseballs and the Jap pellet is the liveliest ever. Only one Jap homer was ever made against us. That was in Yokohama, off Gomez's pitching, and over a short fence. Lefty got to laughing about the big lead we had and tossed up a cripple.'

Lou said the Japanese pitchers were his 'cousins' — his nickname for any pitcher that was easy to hit.

The year of 1932 was the Yankees' year — as well
as the time of Gehrig's high-water achievement of
home-run hitting.

The team went through the season without being
once shut out. Lou himself brushed up his batting
average to .349. In the home run records, Lou hit
thirty-four times for the circuit, twelve less than the
1931 season. But he was a main cog in the machine
that brought the league pennant back and then
pulled the Yanks through the World Series against the
Chicago Cubs in four straight games. Lou was the top
hitter in the series — .529 for the four games and
three home runs, two in one game. It was like the old
days of 1927 and 1928.

But as always, Ruth, with his indomitable showmanship, took the day with his eternally famous
point-the-finger-there-she-goes-boys gesture — hitting a home run exactly where he said. Lou was in
the shadow again.

During these days, Lou appeared more than once
on the non-sporting pages of the newspapers. He had
always been a lover of pets. In his home with Christina in Westchester, he had a parrot, two canaries, a
small German dog, and a big black German police
hound. The latter was brought from Germany and
understood only German. Lou would never tell anyone its name on the theory that the dog would be
spoiled.

In October, he entered the German police in the Bronx County Kennel Club show and won first place. Its name, according to the pedigree, was Afra of Cosalta.

In the same month, Lou refused to campaign for President Herbert Hoover. Although he voted for him, Lou declared that he had 'no intention of becoming a politician.'

He was also sued for the second time in 1932. He had been sued a few years back by the fraternity of Phi Delta Theta at Columbia on the ground that he owed them seventy-three dollars for room and board, but it had been thrown out of court on the ruling that Lou was then a minor.

This time Lou was sued by Mrs. Anna Stelzle of Dudley, Massachusetts. She alleged that she had been hurt in a car driven by Christina and wanted forty thousand dollars in damages. The claim was disallowed by a supreme court jury, but Lou almost missed keeping up his string of consecutive games because of it.

He was still bruising himself in making his impossible tries. During the season he had run after a fly ball and had fallen head over heels into a field box. Any other man would have broken his neck, but as John McGraw once sourly put it, 'To hurt Gehrig you'd have to run over him with a locomotive.' Lou picked himself up without assistance and finished the game. He looked all right outwardly, but for some time afterward suffered from hemorrhages of the shin.

Yet these injuries, like the countless scars he had on his ankles from the sliding spikes of other players, never seemed to hurt his playing ability. Doc Painter, club trainer for the Yankees, was asked for his opinion on the durable Dutchman.

If all ballplayers were like Gehrig [said Doc] there wouldn't be any job for trainers like me on ball clubs. I've been with the team for five years now and during that time I don't believe I have been asked to give Lou — or have given him — more than five rubdowns. When he does ask for attention it is almost apologetically as if he were imposing on me.

My one duty with Gehrig is to see that he is supplied with chewing gum before the start of each game. At the beginning of the season he gives me money for a couple of cartons of the cud and I dole it out a stick at a time, placing it on top of his locker immediately after I report for duty each day.

Gehrig has lasted so long and held up wonderfully because he takes intelligent care of himself. While he doesn't pamper himself any, he doesn't let a minor injury go. Moreover, he follows his personal physician's advice religiously and pays particular attention to his diet. He sees to it that he gets the proper amount of sleep each night, too.

That mention of gum by Doc Painter deserves additional attention. It was Lou's one superstition — besides the smoothing of the dirt before first base at a critical moment. Doc got two dollars each season and bought forty packs. One stick a day to Lou, two on double-header days. Nor would Lou take any gum from anybody else.

The only healthful keep-in-shape prescription that Lou ever took up and discarded was golf. Late in 1932, he took up the game under the tutelage of George Hughes, a New York pro. He wanted to play with Babe Ruth.

Lou caught on immediately and became enthusiastic. Soon he was shooting in the low eighties and doing about fifty-four holes a day. But then he found that in 1933 he suffered a slump, that his batting swing was impaired at the start of the season.

Lou immediately gave golf up. His only recreation became bridge or billiards — at which he had a touch light enough to be amazing when his bulk is considered.

By now Lou Gehrig's fabulous ability to recover from the worst of physical vicissitudes was becoming a sport byword as his hitting had before. In the years to come, up to the time when he was stricken with disease, he was to be known as the man nothing could faze.

From his initiation into the Yankees to the end of 1933 he had trained himself to take it. From 1933 to the end of his career the Durable Dutchman demonstrated that he had trained himself well for the worst and the best in mental as well as physical hard knocks.

☯

Kid Lou

FRANKLIN P. ADAMS, the F. P. A. of columning fame, once jocularly described Lou Gehrig as 'the guy who hit all those home runs the year Ruth broke the record.'

It was a joke, tossed off to fill out a column, but it cut Lou. All the more because it really represented the public's viewpoint of Lou. Lou was the Yanks' Iron Wheelhorse. He did his stint and was universally respected for it. He was never hated or loved the way the Babe was. The crowd expected him to step up and lam the ball, no more. The fact that Lou did just that — and no more — made him an old reliable but not a favorite.

'When I go to bat people are still talking about what Ruth has done,' said Lou without bitterness. 'If I stood on my head and held the bat in my teeth none of the fans would pay the slightest attention to me. But I'm not kicking.'

Nor did he. Cracks like that of F. P. A. might cut
him, but they never left an open wound. Lou idolized
the Babe all his life and never resented a minute of
glory that the Babe stole from him. He never complained about the second-hand aura that encom-
passed his own head.

As a matter of fact, Lou never held the headlines
but three times in his life. Two of those were caused
by sickness — once when he halted his all-time record
of games played, again when the true nature of his
disease was discovered. The last time he held the
spotlight of the press was when he was dead — and
it was a little late then for headlines to make any difference to the Durable Dutchman.

But there were times when Lou, the spectacularly
unspectacular, had his moments of true baseball
grandeur, when he scaled the utmost heights of fame
without fanfare and only those intimately associated
with the game — the writers who had to subordinate
his feats to more newsworthy events, the players
who had no voice except the muttered congratula-
tions of the clubhouse, the managers and owners
who said, 'Come what may, the Kid will never be
traded' — only those knew the greatness of Lou
Gehrig.

He had his day. There was that day — probably
the greatest day — on June 3, 1932, at Philadelphia,
when he hit those four gargantuan home runs.

Credit for this went almost unnoticed in the public eye. It got into the papers simply because it was an integral part of the Yankee victory — not because it was a feat in itself comparable to nothing else in baseball.

Part of this was due to bad publicity breaks. Lou had the knack of doing supremely the right thing for baseball — at the wrong time for the papers.

He was pushed aside in almost a casual manner. In the record of that game at Shibe Park, the story of the contest, written in the aftermath of the game, reflected exactly the mood of those who saw it:

'It was a game in which almost everything happened, and even Gehrig's four homers weren't surprising.'

That was the tone in which the story was written in the *New York Herald Tribune*. Lou surprised no one by his almost legendary feats. Even the notes to the game dismissed him.

'Gehrig got a little monotonous with his homers, but Tony Lazzeri varied his attack ...'

Tony even drove in the same number of runs as Gehrig!

Lou was used to such casual dismissal. The crowning blow to any glory that might have accrued to him on that day came when the papers got the news that John McGraw, wily manager of the Giants for thirty years, had resigned the same day.

Of course that got all the space and no one — except a few scribes, long after — discussed the Iron Horse's willow-wielding.

Then there was that day, the first of October, that same year, the year that was the most satisfying of all years to Lou's heart, that he and Ruth single-handed defeated the Chicago Cubs in the third game of the World Series in Chicago.

Ruth stole the show as he could not help doing. It was the greatest moment, possibly, of Ruth's life too — certainly it was the most dramatic moment of that fading star's career. But Lou came in for his own as well, batting as cleanup man.

Again, let the record speak:

> The Cubs threw caution to the winds today and the third game of the World Series with it, the Yankees winning, 7 to 5. Stung by the thought that too many bases on balls might have cost them the first two contests, the Cubs went out determined to pitch to the batters and make them hit, but they never realized what hitting Babe Ruth and Lou Gehrig were capable of producing.
>
> The mighty Ruth twice drove the ball into the bleachers and out of the park for home runs and Gehrig sounded a Ruthian echo after each....

Always Ruth and Gehrig, the capable firm of Murderers' Row, able to break up and win a ball game between them. But never Gehrig and Ruth. The names, even now, sound a little queer in such juxtaposition. Credit is there for Lou, but not color.

The flame burns steadily in one man, but the spark in the other is the more adored.

Lou was in there with as much power, with as many hits, as Ruth, but the drama was all the Babe's. It was 'Casey at the Bat' to the life — except there was no lack of joy in the Mudville that was New York, for the mighty Babe did not strike out.

> The very first time he came to bat in the opening inning, there was confidence in his manner as he stepped up to the plate. He paused to jest with the raging Cubs, pointed to the right-field bleachers and grinned.... With a step forward, a lurch of his massive shoulders, and a sweep of the celebrated bat, Ruth drove the ball high into the temporary bleachers that had been erected beyond the right-field fence. Upward and onward the ball flew, a white streak that was outlined against the bright blue sky, and the first three Yankee runs romped home.

Gehrig's home run came in the third inning — second of the series — but there was nobody on base. No one booed or jeered Gehrig. He was in there doing his job, and even the Chicago fans respected him for it.

Again the Babe came up, this time in the fifth inning, the score tied. One was out:

> As the Babe moved toward the plate, swinging three bats over his shoulder, a concerted shout of derision broke in the stands. There was a bellowing of boos, hisses, and jeers. There were cries of encouragement for the pitcher, and from the Cub's dugout came a storm of abuse leveled at the Babe.
>
> But Ruth grinned in the face of the hostile greeting. He laughed back at the Cubs and took his place supremely con-

fident. A strike whistled over the plate and joyous outcries filled the air, but the Babe held up one finger as though to say:

'That's only one, though. Just wait.'

Two balls went by, then another strike. The stands rocked with delight. The Chicago players hurled their laughter at the great man but Ruth held up two fingers and still grinned, the super-showman.

On the next pitch the Babe swung. There was a resounding report like the explosion of a gun. Straight for the center-field fence the ball flew on a line. Johnny Moore [the Cub center-fielder] raced back with some vague idea of catching it but suddenly stopped short and stared as the ball sailed on, clearing the farthest corner of the barrier and dropping out into the street 436 feet from home plate.

Before Ruth left the plate and started his swing around the bases, he paused to laugh at the Chicago players, suddenly silent in their dugout. As he rounded first, he flung a remark at Grimm, the Cub first-baseman, as he turned second he tossed a jest at Herman (the Cub second-baseman), and his shoulders shook with satisfaction as he trotted on.

The Babe had done the most melodramatic thing in any sport. He had called his shot and made it good. The day was his. It did not matter that Gehrig, immediately afterward, hit the first ball that came in to him for a home run into the right-field bleachers. Ruth had his two hands around the heart of every fan in the park.

Lou's big grin had been the first to greet the Babe as he came home; his hands with their formidable grip had been the first to squash those of the Babe. He had said fervently, 'I sure will,' to the Babe's panting admonition to 'go out there and do the same,' and he had done it. He had called his shot too, had Lou, but he had not played up to the stands. Lou was not the showman. He was merely a great ballplayer who adored the Babe as much as any tyro fan.

Lou had fallen under the Babe's spell early. Just after he left Hartford and joined the Yanks for good, Lou got a double lesson: how careful the big-leaguers were with anything that might make them good hitters, and how close to Colonel Ruppert's heart the Babe was. The fact that this used to be one of Lou's favorite stories illustrates how little of malice or envy the big fellow had in his heart.

As usual it was on the Babe. The Bam had borrowed a new bat from one of his Yankee team-mates and the first time up had smashed a triple. It was a special bat made of four sections of wood glued together — a type that has since been banned. The Babe immediately sent out a rush order for a dozen more bats of the same fifty-four-ounce weight and type.

A few hours later the genial Colonel Ruppert came bustling around to see his 'boys.' The Babe walked up to him swinging the bat.

'I just ordered a dozen of these, Colonel,' he boomed.

'Fine,' said Ruppert, looking properly blank.

'They cost six dollars apiece,' explained Babe. The Colonel nodded blandly.

'I guess we'll just have to put them in the safe with the rest of the mortgages,' he said, and clapped the Babe on the back.

That was like the Colonel. Babe Ruth was his favorite, although he had a quarrel with him every spring on signing up. He never particularly cared for the retiring Lou. Ed Barrow, wise and bushy-browed, was Lou's real and closest friend on the Yanks. The Babe had his spats out with the Colonel in person — and got eighty thousand dollars as his top salary — whereas Lou usually depended upon Ed to finish off the negotiations and never even hit half the Babe's top.

There were moments, however, when Lou somehow felt life was right and that he was getting more than was really due him, that his cup was overflowing to drowning. Even though he was playing champion second fiddle to Ruth, he was achieving his records by the slow steady process of working at them. Others got them sporadically and spasmodically, but Lou realized that his particular method of climbing the mountain was slow-and-steady, not the quick sprint.

One moment when Lou thrilled to his own power was just before a World Series with the Pittsburgh Pirates; Huggins quietly ordered the Babe and

Gehrig to step out on the field and warm up their bats.

'See that grandstand?' asked Huggins, pointing. The two Princes of Punch nodded.

'See those upper bleachers?' asked Hug. They nodded again.

'I want to see how many of these nice, new, unblemished baseballs you can drop in those stands,' said Huggins. He winked and jerked his head at the Pirate dugout, where the opposition was watching, puzzled.

The Babe and Lou got the idea; they were to do a little psychological intimidation. Hug was renowned for that. First the Babe strolled up to the plate and signaled for a pitch. The bludgeon swung, the ball boomed out and landed in the upper bleachers. Again and again the Bambino let go with all his power. Six balls went caroming into the spot specified by Huggins.

Then Lou stepped up and into the pitched ball. Five times he swung with the coiled-spring power of his chunky legs and great shoulders, and five times the balls went soaring into the same place.

The Pirate bench stirred amazedly. They were seeing the two greatest batters in the world in action. Here, in practice, they were reaching a point in the grandstand where the Pirates never believed a baseball could be carried by a Western Union messenger boy, much less batted.

The Yankees won the series in four straight games.

In the long run, Lou's career held few of the instantaneous thrills that so often mark sports careers. His thrills were cumulative, laid up for him over a period of time, and perhaps all the more satisfying because of it.

In 1931, he was in the midst of home-run rivalry with the mighty Babe. Neither of them had any but the friendliest feelings. Lou's filial affection for the Bambino only increased when one day Babe accosted him on the field.

'Look, Lou,' he confided, pointing. 'Thar's gold behind them thar fences. We're hitting for them and we make money. There's no sense in us fighting against each other and making copy for the papers. Let's do it the sensible way.'

They did do it that way. Lou ended the year in a deadlock with the Babe. Each had forty-six home runs. Lou might have won the coveted title that year and gone on to even higher honors the next season except for a peculiar incident which robbed him of his forty-seventh home run. In this game the ebullient Lyn Lary was on base for the Yanks when Lou hoisted the pellet over the fence for a home run.

Lyn, rounding third from second, suddenly got the idea that the right-fielder had caught Lou's hard-hit ball. Two were out, so Lyn deserted the base paths and trotted over to the Yankee dugout in spite of gestures and shouts that urged him on.

Even then Lou might have saved his record by
some quick thinking. But Locomotive Lou never
was quick on the mental trigger. He had hit a ball
over the fence. His job was to get home. He crossed
the home plate, but his home run was null and void.

In passing Lary on the base paths, Lou had automatically tagged him for the third out. The inning
was already officially over, by the scorekeeper's card,
when Lou put foot on the home plate's rubber.

Lou's apparent genius for coming in second all his
life could almost be counted a record in itself. In
1930 he was second to Al Simmons in batting by two
points. That same year he was tied with Al for second
place to Cronin as the League's most valuable player.
For three successive years prior to 1937 — the year
he finally won it — Lou was runner-up to the most-
valuable-player award. He was always second in the
limelight, second in salary, and second in popular
esteem to Ruth. Most of his records came in two
mighty years, 1927 and 1932, but those were only
two years out of fourteen galling ones — galling, that
is, to all but Lou, who was blissfully happy doing his
job.

He was happy when he hit four home runs in a
World Series — in 1928 — and then went on to hit
three in 1932 and two in 1936. Again when he clipped
the ball for an average of .545 in the 1928 series and
for .529 in the 1932 series. The trouble, as ever, with

these feats was that the Babe always tied or excelled them, yet that never seemed to worry Lou. He had done his own job, and he refused to worry about any statistical betterings.

Incidentally, in seven World Series Lou had a fielding average at first base of .997 — which meant, broken down, that for six of the series, a total of 30 games, he accepted 272 chances and 10 assists without a single error — and only made one error in the seven-series total of 34 games, taking 309 chances and 12 assists. On the basis of his World Series performances and his everyday excellence, Lou was chosen on the All-Star team six times from 1927 to 1939.

Lou was foremost in team power hitting. An example of that is the record which shows that up to Lou's retirement in 1939 American League teams had hit three home runs in an inning only twenty-nine times since the League's foundation. The Yanks had done it twelve times, and out of those twelve Lou had been one of the three hitters nine times.

There was the time on May 22, 1930, too, when Lou — like the Babe, again, who did it just before on May 21 — achieved another high-water mark in his career. He hit three home runs in a day against the Athletics. It was the third time in his career that he had done it. It was one of the few times that any batter has accomplished this triple-triple-homer. Even the mighty Bambino only did it twice.

'Gee,' panted Lou, coming in after the third home run on that third day. 'I think there's a record here some place, but I wouldn't know about it. What does the score-card say?'

Thrills like that were always dropping in Lou's lap from the sound of 'Play ball!' In one day, a couple of months later, the Yanks' Iron Horse hit a double, a triple, and two home runs in four trips to the plate.

There were All-Star team selections, six times in fifteen years, and Most Valuable Player selections in 1927, 1931, 1934, and 1936, but these were honors that seemed unwon — honors that were received gratefully but a little wonderingly by Lou, who had always worked bitterly hard for what he had got and was not accustomed to blue ribbons without toil.

In the way of fielding there was a thrill for Lou in 1928, when, on May 6, he came up with a feat that is still considered quite something, for a first-baseman. Unassisted, he completed two double plays against the Chicago White Sox. More encouraged by this than by any of the long-range hits he had blasted out, Lou, on June 12, proceeded to hit two triples, two home runs and walked once in five times at bat.

'The biggest kick, I think, is in fielding,' Lou once said. 'Maybe because you feel so smooth and right when you pull a good play. But if I had to talk about the kicks I get out of batting, I would say that a nice

Texas Leaguer, calculated to the right distance and
falling where you want it — that would be swell. I
can think how Willie Keeler felt who could hit 'em
where they ain't. Sluggers like me just belt them out
on a line and hope that a fielder won't be in the way.'

That wasn't quite fair. Lou, by this time, had developed into a good place hitter, and knew a great
deal about the various parks in which he played.
The Babe unselfishly coached him on where to put
the ball where it would make the most in bases, and
Lou profited from his advice. From it he got a record:
hitting six consecutive home runs in six consecutive
games, equaling the feat of Ken Williams in 1922.

There were other times of rejoicing in Lou's bosom
at his prowess in baseball. His pet record — runs
batted in — was one of them. He led the league in
1927, 1930, 1931, and 1934. He tied Ruth in 1928.
For thirteen successive seasons he batted in a hundred or more runs.

But all this was not enough. Lou was doomed, by
the bashful quirk in his character, to be unable to
scale the same heights of popularity as the Babe.
To the players he was better liked, to the umpires,
managers, and newspapermen who studied the game
he was a greater figure. But to the crowd — and it
is the crowd that always counts in baseball — he
was second always to the Babe.

One sports commentator, trying his best to cleave

through the fog that surrounded the two greatest figures in modern baseball, trying to figure up their differences to the public that amounted to over forty thousand dollars in salary per year and lucrative cheers and boos for one and penurious respect for the other, said:

'Gehrig is only a great baseball player. Ruth was and is ... a great figure. A Gehrig home run is only a perfect mechanical job. A Ruthian strike-out is a magnificent bit of frustrated effort.'

Perhaps that was it. At any rate, second fiddle played a tune that Lou might not have liked to hear, but he had trained himself to enjoy it. After his marriage, he tried to play first fiddle as well as first base but it never came naturally to him. In those days the Babe was gone from the Yankees and the full light of fame was on Lou.

He tried to live up to it. He doffed his cap and grinned as they cheered him as Yankee captain; he stopped parking his car modestly in a little nook, dark and remote, under the Stadium. Instead he moved it up in front and came in to the sound of huzzas. The Gehrigs held little parties.

In one instance, there was a cocktail party in 1936 at a New York hotel where all the sports writers sat about and sipped drinks, uneasily watching the uneasy Lou as he went from group to group, glad-handing them all. They knew that the whole thing had been advised by Christy Walsh, Lou's new manager, but they had their doubts. As one columnist wrote:

> It came as something of a surprise and a shock when he issued invitations during the winter to a tea at the Commodore. It didn't sound like Lou at all. But the boys gathered, as much out of sheer curiosity as anything else, wondering what Lou was up to. As it turned out, he wasn't up to anything in particular. He was just giving a party for the baseball writers, a sort of informal get-together.
>
> Of course it was all very pleasant and entertaining, but I'm afraid that it didn't serve its purpose, if that purpose was to popularize Lou with the men who write about him. Lou didn't have to seek popularity by throwing a party. He had it already, naturally. And the tea seemed so affected, a little hypocritical, that the boys went away wondering if perhaps Lou hadn't been ill-advised. . . .

Lou read that, and never had another such party.

In the Damon and sub-Pythias combination of Ruth and Lou, there was, as agreed, little contention for publicity honors. The only time that there seemed to be a break — which was really cooked up by sports-writers — was the time when the Babe reportedly said peevishly that Lou was cutting his major-league career short by playing in every game. He declared that even old Piano-Legs couldn't hope to stand up under the licking that churning around the bases every day would give his underpinnings.

Lou replied that he was paid to play every day. He added that he stayed in the lineup on the judgment of the manager and that he was there because he could be of use to them. If he wasn't any use, Lou said, he would get out. And years later he backed up his own words by action.

In lifetime averages, Lou was second to the Babe in batting by a single point. Lou had .340 for his full career, the Babe had .341. In home runs, the Babe was tops. He blasted out 714 during his baseball days; Lou scored 494. Lou hit ten home runs in World Series games, the Babe hit fifteen. Babe led the league in home runs ten times; Lou headed the list twice; they tied for the lead once. Four times Lou was runner-up to the Babe.

Of course Lou had compensation. He was the consistent leader in the runs-batted-in department. He was batting champion of the American League in 1934 — an honor which the Babe attained ten years earlier. But he lacked the showmanship that the Babe had naturally, even when he duplicated the Babe's feats.

Even the naming of Lou the most valuable player in the American League for 1927 passed almost unnoticed in the public prints.

When Ruth began to fade, in 1934, Lou should have come up. It was generally agreed, and Lou himself admitted, that 1934 was his best year in organized ball — though not his most spectacular. Yet there was still Ruth, issuing a flaming ultimatum to Ruppert and McCarthy. And there was the great Dizzy

Dean, boasting of the feats he would perform and
astounding the sporting world by performing just
those feats.

In 1935 Lou went into a slump, just after the Babe
left the Yanks. It would not have been a slump for
most ballplayers, since Lou hit .329, but for a man
who had a lifetime average of .344 up until then, it
was a bad year. To make it worse, the Yanks col-
lapsed in the final stretch in the fall and lost the
pennant.

By 1936, Lou began to receive more recognition.
Before the season both McCarthy and Lou's wife
worked on him, finally convincing him that he was
not a washout, that he could play with the best of
them, and that 1936 was going to be the best in his
life.

'It was a relief,' said Ed Barrow, who pinch-hit
for Joe McCarthy during the times when that worthy
despaired. 'You know how Lou always was. If he
hit, he was happy as a sparrow. If he didn't, he
didn't say a word. Well, all during those days, he
was sunk. Wouldn't talk; even his appetite fell off.
But he came around.'

During 1936 the Yankees cinched the league pennant at the earliest date in the history of the American League. It was done on September 9. McCarthy
wanted to win one hundred and three games that
year and the team did its best, but fell one short.

Most of the credit for this spectacular drive went to Lou. He ran his string of consecutive games to 1808 and for the eleventh season he scored more than a hundred runs. For the fifth time he drove out more than forty home runs and he topped driving in a hundred and fifty runs for the sixth time.

More than that, for the first time he was unchallenged for home-run honors. He won the title with forty-nine, tying his previous record of 1934.

In the World Series against the Giants, however, the second-run luck that always seemed to dog Lou again caught up to him. For a time he was the hero of the series when he hit a home run off Carl Hubbell, one of the greatest pitchers of all time, to score two runs. But then the jinx scored.

In the fifth game, the Yankees were riding on the tide of victory, leading three to one in games, when Lou lost the game. He had singled in the second inning and when another ball was hit to Mel Ott in the outfield. Mel had momentarily fumbled it. On this error, Lou pounded around to third.

Dickey hit a hard drive to the infield and tore down the first-base line. On third, caught in one of those inexplicable lapses of action that sometimes overwhelmed him, Lou stood indecisive for a split second. Then, too late, he put his mighty legs in action and churned homeward.

He had waited too long. Dickey was thrown out at

first and the ball had whizzed back to the plate. Lou was out, ending the inning, and the Giants won, 5 to 4.

The Yankees won the next game and with it the series, four games to two, but Lou was as nearly the goat as any member of a winning team could be.

○

Durable Lou

IT WAS obvious from the beginning of Lou Gehrig's baseball career that his most impressive contribution to the sport, next to his example of modesty and clean living, would be his persistence.

He never for a moment, in his stubborn Dutch way, doubted that he would reach the top. And he never relaxed for a moment in his drive to get there.

Lou would work over his fielding for hours. When his hitting sagged, he would ask advice of everyone, including Tim Sullivan, the Yankee bat boy, and then go out on the field and try every stance and panacea that had been offered him. He would memorize the plays that Miller Huggins and Joe McCarthy outlined to him until they hurt. No effort was too great to bring him to the top.

Yet Lou put so much upon his body that is was doubtful if he could have done as much if he had had less magnificent physical equipment. The doctors always claimed that his sturdy neck, powerful legs, and stocky torso formed an almost ideal combination for a power-hitting ballplayer. And Lou's shoulders, as square and powerful as brick gables, put the last touch on their opinion.

By exercise and drive Lou built himself to what he was. There is no better illustration of how this came about than the one of his early days in Hartford.

When Lou was put there by Miller Huggins to get spice and seasoning, O'Connor, the Hartford manager, felt a bit put out over Lou's presence. For a long while he pulled at his thinning hair, and he ruined half a dozen of his best baseball caps by stamping on them with his spikes.

It seems that Huggins had left explicit orders that the big Columbia hitter was to be kept on first base exclusively — and the orders went. O'Connor did keep him there. But Lou was webfooted around the first sack and his hitting was pathetic in the extreme. He was mooning over the fact that the Yanks had farmed him out and his big German countenance was continually sunk in gloom.

O'Connor could do nothing with him.

'What's the matter, kid?' he would plead with Lou in the clubhouse. 'You sick or something?'

But Lou would shake his head and go out on the field and dub away another ball game.

So O'Connor held on to his sanity with both hands until one Friday. On that particular day Lou struck out three times in succession. Howling, O'Connor rushed to the nearest Western Union office and sent a wire, telling the whole story to Huggins in an ample night letter. He was fed up and he wouldn't keep that lug from college on the team another minute no matter if he lost his job over it.

No answer came to the wire. The reason was that Huggins never went to the Yankee headquarters. That particular Saturday the Yanks were playing out of town.

So O'Connor, without any authority to remove Lou, was forced to put the big stocky kid in at first base again for Saturday's game. Inwardly seething, O'Connor watched, prepared to see Hartford drop another game over Lou's misdemeanors at bat and on the field.

Something inside Lou snapped that day. His policy of persistent learning broke through and left him swinging with the deadly accuracy of a machine. He caught one ball on the nose and it went over the fence to win the ball game.

O'Connor was speechless and suspicious. He said nothing. Sunday Lou went into the game again, for no answer to O'Connor's telegram had arrived. The bill was a double-header.

Lou's hitting broke up both games. His continued

trying had at last paid dividends. His errors didn't matter. As the last out was recorded, O'Connor was seen to leave the dugout in a trail of dust for the nearest telegraph office. There he hastily gabbled a message to the operator and streaked back to the clubhouse. He found Lou, as usual, soaping himself in the shower.

O'Connor waited until Lou got out. Then he stuck out his hand.

'Put it right there,' he announced beamingly. 'I knew you could hit all the time.'

This quality of stick-to-itiveness that finally won around everyone who ever had anything to do with Lou Gehrig, was apparent even in his extra-curricular activities.

There was that story, perhaps the most famous story about Lou, of his radio broadcast. The script had been carefully built up by the sponsors, the makers of Huskies, a potent breakfast-food, to the point where Lou's recommendation of their product would come in.

Knowing Lou's mike-nervousness, the writers had fixed the program so that it was written around him. He only had to say one word in the whole program.

At the appointed time Lou was at the microphone, sweating gently, but ready for his one-word broadcast. He heard the announcer eulogize his work, review his feats of the past few years, and then pause.

'Lou is here in the studio, and I would like to ask him to what he owes his tremendous strength and endurance,' said the announcer mellifluously. He turned to the paling Lou.

'To what *do* you owe your present marvelous physical condition?' he asked blandly.

The answer in the script was, of course, 'Huskies.' But Lou had no thought for the script. He throttled the microphone with a sweat-filled hand and piped nervously: 'Wheaties.'

That happened to be the name of Huskies' most formidable rival in the breakfast-food field.

The laughter that followed the broadcast was heard from coast to coast. Sports writers and players kept wigging Lou about it for weeks. Lou, thoroughly miserable at what he considered his poor showing, returned the check for five hundred dollars that he had received for the broadcast.

The sponsors, however, realizing that they had received a thousand times more value in publicity from the incident, returned the check again to Lou with a note: 'Every ballplayer is entitled to three strikes.' It is an ironic coincidence that the broadcast in 1939, on July 4, when Lou had his great day at the Yankee Stadium, was sponsored by Wheaties.

Lou's habit of plugging perfection made him stay close to baseball business. He thought, ate, drank, lived, and slept it.

Because of this he was never even very good at kidding the other players. The measure of his humor was in a remark he made to the Babe one day. The Bam was chewing one of his customary huge quids of tobacco and Lou remonstrated.

'Hey, Babe,' he said gently. 'That's a pretty big quid. I bet it would tire a mouse just to run around it when you spit it out.'

By the same token Lou trained himself to take it. On one occasion, when the Yankee team was returning from a series of exhibition games in Canada, they were stopped at the border by immigration agents who asked if they had any contraband.

'Sure,' said Lefty Gomez, the goofy Castilian pitcher.

'What?' said the amazed customs and immigrations men. 'Where?'

Lefty's team-mates watched him in amazement.

'Dope,' said Gomez.

'Dope?' chorused everyone.

'Sure,' said Gomez, pointing to the broad-grinning Lou. 'Right there. More than two hundred and ten pounds of it.'

On another occasion Lefty cheered up Lou no little. It was the fateful day after he had returned from the Mayo Clinic with the bad news of his oncoming paralysis. He was sitting in the dugout, glum and unresponsive, when Lefty came up to him with his hands behind his back.

'Say, Lou,' said Lefty, who had recently returned
from an operation at Johns Hopkins in Baltimore,
'you may think those sawbones up in Minnesota are
some stuff. But look what they took out of my arm
in Baltimore.' He abruptly produced a huge soup-
bone from behind his back.

Lou could tell stories on himself. One of his
favorites, so old that it has whiskers on it, deserves
repeating here because Lou recited it at the *Herald
Tribune* Forum in 1938. And he told it on himself.
This is the actual transcript.

> Our club had come into St. Louis to play a series, and as
> we got off the train and trooped through the waiting-room
> on the way to our hotel, a lot of people recognized us and
> stopped to stare.
>
> I happened to pause at the newsstand to buy a paper and
> a little old lady was standing there beside me. She touched
> me on the arm and asked if I knew who all those men were
> that everyone was looking at.
>
> I said, 'Why, yes, lady. Those are the Yankees.'
>
> She said, 'The Yankees? What do they do?'
>
> I said they played baseball. 'Is that all?' she said, and
> when I nodded, she added, 'Tch, tch! They ought to be
> ashamed of themselves — big, strong men like that playing
> games. They ought to go to work.'

Perhaps that amused Lou because it reflected the
opinion of his mother and father. Christina still
liked to remind callers to the home that Lou was
called Columbia Lou because he had been a college
man. They still thought that baseball was not anything that a grown man could be quite proud of
playing for a living.

But then in the sense that he always believed devoutly in the copybook adages and lived cleanly and without ostentation, Lou was always one of those players who never really grew up. In a New York paper one day in February, 1930, there was a little note:

It certainly was a treat to open this morning's paper and see the Reg'lar Fellers cartoon staring at me. I have always enjoyed and admired this strip because of its originality and its clean, wholesome humor. Several friends of mine also passed favorable comment and I believe the paper is to be congratulated on obtaining this strip.

The letter was signed Lou Gehrig. The Iron Horse had no publicity man or manager — off the field — in those days. It was not a stunt to attract attention. Lou honestly felt that way, and the pomposity that such a letter might have meant in another person was utterly lacking in him.

Letters were not the only bits of writing he could do. Few pieces were ghosted for him. Those that were had to bear his corrections and notes, and usually these added to their value. In 1932 Lou took time out at the St. Petersburg training camp in Florida and covered an amateur sports writers' game. The article appeared under his by-line and the whole piece was not without its own humor:

... Here it was the ninth inning with two out and the Yankee writers four runs behind the Brooklyn scribes, as they call themselves for what reason I don't know. Buck

O'Neil of the *Journal,* who has called me a dumb base-runner more than once, was on first base and what does he do but try and steal second.

Sure he was thrown out. A guy can't run that long in one place and not be thrown out....

Lou was always considered the spark-plug of the Yankees during his playing days. This was one of the prime considerations that made Joe McCarthy appoint him to be captain of the team in 1935. He was always 'talking it up,' whether on the field or from the dugout or coaching box. Rarely, if ever, did he 'jockey' the boys on the opposing team. Lou preferred to hold his chatter down to encouraging his own team.

One year the Yanks were having a crucial series with Detroit. The loss of one game might mean that the Tigers would go catapulting into first place and the whole series might be lost — and with it the pennant.

Red Ruffing, the famous relief pitcher and a huge man himself on the field and at bat, was pitching. The bases were filled and Hank Greenberg, the home-run hitter, was at bat. Lou ambled over to Ruffing and patted him on the back.

'Come on, Red,' he said, 'we're all ready and willing to go, all behind you. You know what to serve up there; give 'em the works.'

At first Red paid no attention, thumping the ball into his mitt and staring into the stands. Then, as

Lou continued to eagerly pour words of advice and reassurance into his ears, Ruffing turned and winked

'Say, Lou,' he said calmly, 'what town are we playing in today?'

It was Lou who was responsible in the main for the smashing victories over the Chicago Cubs in four straight games in the World Series of 1932. Mark Koenig, the former Yank short-stop, had been traded to the Cubs in mid-season and had played sensational ball in fifty-eight games, and, as Lou thought, had virtually won the pennant for them by his fielding and stick work.

It was with quite a shock, therefore, when the Cubs met to vote the shares in the forthcoming World Series that Lou heard that Koenig had been voted only a half share because he had been with the team only a half-season.

Lou, who had played in the same infield with Koenig for years, liked him as an individual and thought him a great player, gathered the Yanks together.

'Look, fellows,' he said. 'Mark's only going to get a half-share of the Cubs' loot. I think they're a bunch of tightwads and misers. We've always wanted to beat other clubs by a hundred to nothing if we could, but this is a special occasion. Let's cut those boys down to nothing and score fifty runs a game and finish it off in four games. Let's ride 'em rough.'

The Yanks did. They didn't make fifty runs a
game, but they scored a record number for any club
in any four-game World Series — thirty-seven —
called their shots, rocketed extra-base hits off the
bleachers, and in general made the Cubs very miserable. The series only went four games, all to the
Yanks, and in the final game the score was the lop-
sided one of 13 to 6. Lou hit three home runs, Ruth
and Lazzeri each two.

Lou was never superstitious about his hitting. He
knew himself too well. If he were slumping, he found
the reason and corrected it all during his career —
except at the end when there was no cure. In one
slump in 1937 he jokingly volunteered the information to friends that practically everybody was worried
about his snapping out of it except himself.

'Everybody's been sending me good-luck charms
lately,' he remarked.

'What sort of charms?' somebody asked.

'Oh, everything. Look: horseshoes, wishbones,
four-leaf clovers, jeep — oh, all sorts of stuff.'

Lou reached in his pocket.

'Money, too,' he said. He pulled out a pre-Roose-
velt dollar bill and a couple of other coins. 'Lots of
people have been sending me lucky pennies, dimes
and two-dollar bills and gold pieces ——'

'Humph!' interrupted McCarthy, who had been
eavesdropping. 'Sounds like it pays you better to be
in a slump than I pay you to hit.'

Lou's record string of games that gave his persistence its most enduring fame was once imperiled by the fact that he was forced to answer a summons for a suit in the supreme court in the afternoon. He sat nervously next to Christina, squirming and wriggling in his chair, looking at the clock, then out the window. From time to time his mother would pat him on the arm: 'There now, Louie.'

The case was for forty thousand dollars damages against himself and Christina as the result of an automobile accident in 1927. He would be forced to wait perhaps until the game was over, and his record depended on his being in the game, at least for the start. Lou had seen to it that neither injury nor time had interfered with his string, but now the law bade fair to do it.

The clock said two-thirty — game starting time. Lou half-rose from his chair. But just then someone came over to him and whispered in his ear. With a smile of beatific satisfaction Lou sank back in his chair. The game between the Yankees and the St. Louis Browns had been called off because of weather.

Out at the Stadium, Ed Barrow, who had called the game, pursed his lips for the reporters and glanced upward under his shaggy brows at the blue and cloudless sky of spring. His sparse hair was ruffled by the breeze.

'Yes sir,' he said. 'I was fooled. I thought this would be a raw, icy day.'

They had no choice but to take his word, but they remembered that he was one of Lou's best friends.

Yet as much as Lou valued his record, his giving it up was as gracious an event as exists in sporting annals. When Babe Dahlgren, his successor, went out in the first game and poled a home run, Lou was the first person to greet him at the plate.

'Gosh, Babe!' Lou cried excitedly. 'Why didn't you tell me you felt that way? I would have got out of here long ago.'

Recalling the moments when he got the biggest kicks out of baseball, Lou always maintained that many of them came from his determination to keep his record going — his record of 2130 straight games played, a mark that is likely to outlast most of the other major league records.

Some times Lou played solely on nerve. He was clipped by wild pitches; in Washington a doctor ordered him out of the game after he had been hit on the head by a ball pitched by speed-king Earl Whitehill, but Lou refused. He proved that he was right, as well, a little later, by hitting a home run that won the game.

Little things like cut or bruised legs from brash runners that came slashing and bouncing into first never bothered Gehrig — the runners got the worst of it, anyway, like hitting a brick wall. At one time he played for a while with a chipped little-finger bone.

His worst enemy, Lou maintained, was lumbago. And his closest shave to having to stop his streak was one day at Detroit in 1934. 'I had to fall out of bed to get up,' said Lou, recalling that his lumbago was so bad that he felt like a corpse with rigor mortis. 'I called Doc Painter, the club trainer, and he dressed me so that I could get to the ball park. Once out there, he had to undress me again and dress me in my uniform so I could go into the game. Joe McCarthy let me lead off the lineup — I was listed as short-stop — and I singled. Then I went back to bed to nurse my back.'

Actually, Lou played in 2156 games during his big-league career, perhaps 2500 if all his games both in the bushes and in exhibitions are counted. His big-league record of 2130 consecutive games excludes the World Series games and exhibitions, but Lou only missed a dozen of the latter in the days of his playing.

There were disappointments to temper the thrills. Lou always felt badly because he only won the American League batting championship once in his life — in 1934 with an average of .363. He came close on several other occasions, but if ever a man realized that close doesn't count, that man was Lou. There was some comfort in the fact that Ruth, too, had won the Championship only once, in 1924, the year before Lou broke into the big leagues with an average of .378.

But these averages could not compare with those compiled by Tyrus Raymond Cobb (who made .420 in 1911 in 146 games) and with that of Sisler, Lou's early idol, who also made .420 in 1922 in 142 games.

In the eyes of the Lou Gehrig fans the chief disappointment was their hero's retiring ways. They always wanted him to come out from under the shade of Babe Ruth's great and colorful personality. Yet Gehrig never felt that way. He was too much an admirer of the Babe's, and never gave his own semi-obscurity a thought.

A little while after Lou retired from active playing he and his wife had a party in New Rochelle. There were the famous suet cookies of Christina and the pickled eels — there was a tradition among the Yankees that anyone who had a slump would come out of it if he could eat a Gehrig eel.

At this party, Lou, as always, served the drinks that he loved to make but never touched himself. One incident, related by a writer who attended, illustrates the two facets of Lou's character that colored even his gigantic persistence — his love of baseball and his eagerness to give the other guy the best he had.

The cocktails that Lou carried around in his big hams were Martinis. As they were passed, one of the players held one up to the light.

'Hey, Lou,' he exclaimed. 'What's this? No olives?'

Lou hastened to explain. 'I don't put 'em in,' he said. 'It gives me a lot more room for gin.' He looked affectionately around the room. 'I want you guys to have a lot of fun,' he said slowly. 'Have some for me, too; I won't be having much any more.'

Mr. Lou

IT IS still a question in the minds of many of Lou Gehrig's baseball friends whether the shy, unassuming giant meant to marry. Certainly the happiest years of his life came after his marriage. Certainly he loved his wife and never regretted the step.

But the idea of Lou's getting married was, for a long time, impossible for those who knew him to conjure up.

There was his love for his mother, a clean-cut Freudian complex that lost its psychological overtones only because Lou made no bones about it.

'All that I am and have I owe to my darling mother' was not an unusual statement for him to make to sports writers — or over the air. The phrasing, which would have sounded affected in anyone else, was sincere and whole-hearted in Lou. His actions all his life proved that much.

Through the years before 1933 when he was making
the name of Gehrig known as a clouting terror, Lou
laughed off all ideas of marriage.

'Me?' he used to say and laugh quietly. 'Not me.
I don't have to. My mother makes a home for me —
good food, good bed — I don't want any more than
my mother gives me.' And he said it so convincingly
that everyone believed him.

Lou occasionally went out with the girls in Yorkville, some that he had grown up with. But no reporter ever caught him. The *New Yorker*, in a sly
profile, planted a rumor that he had been seen with a
mysterious 'red-cheeked German girl who wore a
bunch of flowers in her hat,' but admitted in the same
sentence that the fact was unverified. Lou himself
denied it.

So it came as a really complete surprise to the
sporting world when on June 17, 1933, two days
before his thirtieth birthday, Lou reddened and admitted to a heckler that he was engaged to be married.

'To whom?' screamed the scribe, not forgetting his
grammar.

'To Eleanor,' mumbled Lou.

'Eleanor who?' demanded the writer, pencil poised.

'Miss Twitchell, of course,' Lou said defiantly.

Eleanor Twitchell was a calm, comely young
woman with brunette hair that fell in soft waves on
either side of her head, with wise brown eyes. She

was, on her record, and on her performance-to-come, the ideal wife for Lou.

She came from Chicago. There she had been the efficient manager and owner of a large apartment house, one of the largest in the Windy City. Her experience as a business woman served her in good stead, because she rapidly became Lou's unofficial business manager — not only that, but also his promoter, encourager, one-woman publicity staff, and backer-up, helpmate in the literal sense of the word.

Lou had met her in Chicago in 1929 amid the sound of crashing stocks and tumbling incomes. While most of the ballplayers were glum-faced at the reports of their fading investments, Lou was stammering before the level gaze of Eleanor.

After the party where Lou met her — Eleanor said later that 'he hardly said a word, just smiled and sat still' — the whole affair seemed dropped. Lou and the Yankees finished their stand with the White Sox and went back to New York. He had enough on his mind keeping his string of games going and keeping his hitting average up with the leaders.

Three years later, in 1932, Lou and Eleanor met again. This time Eleanor made an ineradicable impression. As the first time, they met at a party at the house of a mutual friend. Lou was still extraordinarily shy, confining his conversation to monosyllables, but following Eleanor around the room with his eyes.

Eleanor remembered Lou quite well. 'It was love at first sight for me again — even though three years had gone by,' she said. She remembered his phobia, how he was afraid a pretty girl might sit by him, and she let Lou come to her. Come he did, like a bashful bear, across the room and asked her if she was busy.

She was not. Eleanor had not quite got over her preconception of Lou as a sort of rube, Lardneresque character — the shy, boyish ways of the ballplayer had given her a rude awakening, although a pleasant one. She wanted to find out more about him.

Lou, in a moment of aberration, tried to start a conversation and subsided into vagueness. She helped him along, but pretty soon Lou fled. 'Good-bye' was the actual extent of his distinguishable words.

Eleanor was in despair. She thought that she might have offended Lou in some way in spite of the reassurance of his friends. She knew she could talk intelligently about baseball but Lou had never given her a chance. So she decided to forget about him.

Lou, however, worked just the other way. A year later, he called her up on the long-distance telephone and actually chatted with her for a few minutes — stopping on the dot as soon as his three minutes were up, true to his German frugality. Neither of them ever remembered a word of what they said.

'It was just polite stuff,' said Lou.

Eleanor went to visit her aunt, a Mrs. Gene Austin, at Freeport, Long Island. By devious ways and means, she managed to let Lou know that she was there and the big ballplayer occasionally dropped in.

By this time there were whispers about Lou's being engaged going around. Some of the weaker players succumbed to them, but those wiseacres who knew Lou best stoutly maintained there was nothing to them.

In Lou's case the rumors were true. But, as Eleanor laughingly disclosed some years later, he never did actually propose to her.

They were sitting on the traditional sofa when Lou began to mutter. He was talking with more than his usual vehemence. His eyes were glassy but pleading.

'Eleanor,' he said rapidly. 'I'm just a ballplayer. Not much good. But I like ballplaying. You like ballplaying.'

He paused.

'Yes,' said Eleanor.

Lou took a deep breath and veered. 'Did you see that game with the Pirates last fall?' he asked.

Eleanor shook her head.

'Well,' said Lou, 'what I meant was ——'

Eleanor took it into her own hands.

'Lou,' she said, putting her hand on his, 'do you really want to tell me something — something that's very serious to both of us?'

Lou nodded mutely.

'Can't you say it?' asked Eleanor gently.

'Well, I ——' said Lou, then subsided into silence again.

'Are you trying to — I know what you want to say,' said Eleanor firmly.

'Do you?' said the amazed Lou.

'Do you want to say you want to marry me?' asked Eleanor, trembling a little.

Lou nodded in relief. 'That's it,' he said with a sigh. Eleanor waited. Lou slid over to her, took her in his arms in a bear hug, planted a hasty kiss on her lips, and fairly ran for the door.

So it was settled. The marriage was planned, without much help from Lou, for the thirtieth of September, two days before the end of the baseball season in 1933. It was a long time away, but Eleanor realized that the first duty of a baseball wife is not to interfere with the career of her husband.

It was to be a rather dressy wedding. Flowers had arrived for the banks of decorations, carpenters and painters were fixing up the home of her aunt. Everything was nearly ready — including the crowds that were already gathering to see the wedding of their hero.

Lou arrived the afternoon before the wedding, white as a shroud. Eleanor said nothing but felt the same qualms — as though it were going to be a marriage in a goldfish bowl.

Lou had come over for the rehearsal, but as his eyes roved wildly about and saw all the finery that he would have to pass through, the flowers, the chairs, the ghostly faces of the guests, the imaginary dude-clothes he would have to wear — his courage that had made him face sickness, poverty, and the greatest pitchers in baseball suddenly failed him. His knees turned to water and he clutched at Eleanor.

'Do we have to go through with all this ceremony, dear?' he said desperately.

'Not if you don't want to,' said Eleanor.

'I don't,' moaned Lou. 'Let's — let's — let's get hold of the mayor — he's my friend. We'll have him marry us right here and now.'

So the mayor of New Rochelle was rounded up and put to good use a day ahead of the ceremony. Amid the curious carpenters and painters, a fringe of urchins and the immediate families, Lou and Eleanor stood before the altar and became man and wife.

Both were so nervous that they hardly lasted through the ceremony. Immediately afterward, Eleanor's knees gave way and she hastily sat down. Lou, his color returning, looked beseechingly at her.

'Are you worried, darling?' she asked.

'I've got a game to play,' he blurted. And so the day ended, with Eleanor sitting weakly on a sofa and Lou rushing off to play baseball.

It was no more than Eleanor was prepared for.

She had been born in Chicago and had attended high
school there, then attended the University of Wis-
consin. Her chief interests had always been music and
psychology. To these she now added baseball.

After marrying Lou she played but little music,
although an accomplished pianist. Lou would often
plead with her to take up playing seriously again, but
she always won the argument by saying:

'What would Bach have to do with bats?'

When he said, 'Why don't you play more, at least
for your own amusement?' her stock reply was, 'For
my own amazement, you mean.'

Her knowledge of psychology stood her well in
working out Lou's career. Pal, as Lou always called
Eleanor, set about in businesslike fashion to give
Lou the place that the Babe had by now vacated.
She knew about baseball from actual playing —
having been a tomboy in the pick-up ball games in
Chicago's sand lots and being a close friend of the
Harry Grabiners, who owned a piece of the Chicago
White Sox. She had other sports interests in golf
and tennis and swimming, as well.

Now she took advantage of every opportunity to
become the perfect baseball wife. She attended every
possible game. She discussed shop with the other
baseball wives who are destined for the playing life
of their husbands to sit behind the dugout during
the baseball season, and stay and knit at home during

the winter when their husbands are away hunting or fishing.

How well Eleanor Gehrig fitted into the task she had laid out for herself is apparent in the fact that Lou always called her 'Pal.' Yet her road was not easy. Christina did not yield any of her rights easily. But before long not only the three of them — Lou, Christina, and Eleanor — were living in harmony, but also Eleanor's mother, to whom he referred in his famous speech of July 4, 1939, on the first Lou Gehrig Day.

The first real problem that Eleanor Gehrig had to overcome for herself was the fact that she was married to a famous man. She had to force herself to realize that Lou did not belong to her entirely — he belonged as well to the baseball public.

'No woman,' she said once, 'likes to have someone directly behind her calling her husband a big yellow bum all day.'

But she became reconciled to it — and even managed to grin when the fans booed the Yankees.

Her first domestic problem came the day after she married Lou. She, of course, had been reading all the papers on Lou that she could beg, borrow, or steal. She knew so little about her husband that she was driven in desperation to take advantage of what the sports writers knew. And the problem was pickled eels.

'One wonders,' ran a piece, 'whether Mrs. Lou
Gehrig, who was Miss Eleanor Twitchell of Chicago,
is as good as Lou's mother at preparing pickled eels,
the favorite dish of the Yankees' famous first-baseman and slugger.'

Eleanor drew a deep breath. She had to cross that
Rubicon, and the sooner the better. She cornered Lou
the day after their marriage — the honeymoon had
been put off in deference to the American League
baseball schedule.

'Lou,' she said, 'are you really very fond of eels?'

'What?' said Lou absently, oiling his glove in the
kitchen.

'Pickled eels,' said Eleanor faintly. 'Are you really
fond of them?'

Lou looked up and grinned. 'Never touch 'em.
Never ate one in my life. Like to catch 'em, though.
Some of the boys — Babe Ruth is one — like them,
but I hate 'em.'

The relief was so great that Eleanor nearly cried.
Lou explained to her that she shouldn't believe
everything she read in the papers that the boys
cooked up. Pickled eels had been a dish at the
Gehrig house for years and a lot of the ballplayers
who didn't like them ate them anyway. There was a
superstition that the eels would snap anybody out of
a hitting slump.

Years later, when Lou was in a slump, he cautiously
tasted one of the pickled eels, but gave it up.

When they were married, the carpenter who was fixing up for the wedding offered the only philosophic comment on the union.

'Gee,' he said, 'this is swell. This is the first time I've ever been to a prominent wedding.'

The rest of the country felt that way, too. By his marriage Lou suddenly jumped more than ever into prominence. The details leading up to the wedding slipped out. How a mutual friend had suggested the wedding; how the engagement had lasted only six months yet how they had known each other six years; and how, on the day the engagement slipped out via the grapevine route, Lou had hit a home run just for his bride-to-be.

Now the baseball fans wanted to know just how things were going with their hero and his chosen wife. Eleanor had given up the apartment house she owned and operated in Chicago — it was becoming too much of a financial liability and Lou took up all of her time anyway. They set up housekeeping in an apartment in the Bronx within easy driving distance of the Yankee Stadium. The reason for its situation was obvious. The reason for its being an apartment was apparent as well. Though Lou had had assurance time and again from the Yankee owners that he was set for life with the New York team, both he and Eleanor realized that the future of a baseball player was more uncertain than that of a Foreign Legionnaire. At any time, without warning, he might be sold or traded to a team anywhere from one hundred to five hundred miles away.

'It seems,' said Eleanor ruefully, 'that I spend most of my time with my head in a trunk.'

She used to cite the way they celebrated anniversaries. For Lou's birthday, she went to Detroit. For the first wedding anniversary, she had to go to Washington. And after the season was over, they launched immediately on a barnstorming trip around the world. Nor was that all. Right after they came home, they were on their way to Florida for a fishing trip, and after that came the training camp of the Yankees at St. Petersburg.

So the life of the Gehrigs fell into a certain routine that they followed, more or less, for the remainder of Lou's career.

There was no night life. Eleanor stayed at home and liked it. She bought only a few evening gowns in her whole life with Lou — and then mostly to admire them at home. Most of her time was spent in sports clothes at the games.

Occasionally, they went to double-feature movies. Lou, before his marriage, had been a movie fan of the first water. He rarely missed a show in town, and the movie-houses were his chief form of relaxation off the ball-field. Now he and Eleanor went together.

Sometimes close friends — the Dickeys, the Barrows, or other members of the team — dropped in and had a chat. But for the most part it was early to bed and early to rise, with little but baseball to occupy either the waking or sleeping hours.

During the baseball season, Eleanor Gehrig rarely traveled with Lou. Both of them agreed that it was too expensive and too much of a strain — especially in the hot summer months — riding in the trains and indulging in the two or three days stand in the various cities. So Eleanor stayed at home in the apartment, did the housework, played the piano, and occasionally did some writing for magazines about her famous husband.

Although she could cook, Eleanor did not try to do much of it. She knew how much Lou enjoyed the cooking of his mother Christina, and she determined to give him as much of that same German food as she could. She hired a fine Yorkville cook and gave him the fare to which he was accustomed.

Even waiting at home for Lou was not much satisfaction for Eleanor. When he did return, she saw little of him — compared to what other wives saw of their go-to-business husbands.

'The major-league baseball season,' she explained, 'lasts six months — about. For three months of that, the team is traveling. That means that Lou is home for two weeks and away for two weeks. Unless it rains, he hasn't a chance of getting a day off.'

So the baseball wife is condemned to two things: the radio and the book of clippings about her husband. Sometimes, as Mrs. Gehrig did, they meet their husbands at various cities through the league — but usually they stay at home.

Even when Lou was home — although he was far better-natured and amenable than most ballplayers — there was not much variety in conversation — for that matter there was not much conversation.

Eleanor knew that discussion of the game was taboo.

'It's an old axiom that a player should leave the field behind him when he comes home,' she said.

But Lou would be playing the game over and over again.

'If we had done this or that,' he would mutter abstractedly, and it was up to Eleanor Gehrig to look up from her book and murmur, 'Yes, dear.'

Mrs. Gehrig always maintained that she could tell instantly whether the Yanks had won or lost a game simply by the expression of Lou's face when he came in. Here are the various signs that she tabulated:

Glum face — Yankees lost.

Chin on chest — No hits.

Thoughtful look — Yankees won.

Beaming, with dimples, 'as though he had swallowed a sunbeam' — a home run.

When Eleanor Gehrig went to the ball-park, she

experienced her most turbulent moments. Unlike the rest of the baseball fans, she always felt that she had to repress her emotions. If Lou hit a home run, the rest of the grandstand might jump to its feet screaming hosannas, but Eleanor remained primly seated most of the time, swelling with pride inside.

On the other hand, if Lou was swinging like a gate, missing easy ones, and the crowd was beginning to get impatient and boo — the strain was a thousand times greater. And when he struck out she usually covered her ears against the jeers and by main strength held herself back from murdering the idiot just behind her who was damning her husband.

To friends, she confided that her most thrilling moments in seeing Lou on the field were three:

1. When Lou went on a hitting rampage in the World Series of 1932. They were not even engaged yet, but Eleanor was in love. She had overcome whatever throbs of dislike she felt for the big fellow who so often managed to beat her then-favorite team, the White Sox, with the main strength of his own bludgeon.

2. The home run he hit in Chicago the day the engagement was made public in 1933.

3. The day in September, 1934, when Lou, on the last day of the season, made three hits out of four at bat. By this feat he nosed out Charlie Gehringer for the batting championship — the only year Lou ever held that prized honor.

During his Iron Horse career, Lou received a number of minor injuries. But the one that frightened Eleanor most was the one which happened in 1934 in an exhibition game at Norfolk, Virginia.

It had been a bruising year for Lou anyway. He had had broken bones, lumbago, sprained fingers, and a half-dozen other ailments, but played on in spite of them. But on June 29 Lou was in the Yankee lineup against Norfolk. Ray White, also an ex-Columbia man, was pitching for the Virginia Tars.

One of his throws, a whistling curve, broke sharply. For once Lou's eye, one of the keenest in the big leagues, was slow. The ball caught him on the side of the head.

Lou staggered, then fell face forward like a felled tree to the ground. He was out cold for five minutes. The doctor who examined him decided that Lou had a brain concussion and ordered him off the field.

Lou went to bed agreeably -- but not before he had firmly announced that he would play the next day, willy-nilly, against the Washington American League team.

The next day he was in the lineup despite everything that could be said or done to dissuade him. He was wearing one of Babe Ruth's size seven and a half caps. It was slit open down the side to accommodate a knob on his head that was as large as an avocado.

That day Lou went to bat three times — and came

up with three triples. But the perverse baseball Fates had something to say about it. Rain cut the game short and Lou's three hits were washed off the record along with the game.

At home Eleanor had just finished helping her mother move into a new apartment. She had heard nothing of the accident; her mother had no telephone as yet. She had no inkling of what had happened at Norfolk until her brother came home at two in the morning with the news. He had seen the item in a paper and had long-distanced Norfolk to find out about it.

'Don't get excited, El,' were his first words. 'Lou's been hurt.'

Her heart sank. She was unable to say a word.

'He was hit on the head with a pitched ball,' her brother went on. He gave her the newspaper. Eleanor grabbed it and read every word over and over again. Her mind was a blank, but pictures were forming — of Lou bruised and dazed, staggering off the field, alone, friendless . . .

'They've been trying to get you by telephone,' said her brother, 'but you weren't in. The team has gone by boat to Washington. He won't get there until nine this morning.'

Eleanor got up at once. She packed and left her mother's apartment and went directly to their home at New Rochelle. There, clad in a thin kimono, she sat up all night waiting for any sort of message that might come through. During those long hours her imagination ran wild: a fractured skull... loss of memory... an idiot... dead....

At nine o'clock, she stifled her sobbing and emptied the ash-tray that was piled high with cigarettes she had smoked during her vigil. After what seemed an interminable wait on the telephone, she managed to get Lou.

'Lou?' she cried. 'Are you all right, dear?'

'Sure,' he said vigorously. 'I'm all right. Don't you worry. I'm all right.'

For a moment Eleanor was reassured. But the morning papers she picked up outside the door had pictures of Lou being carried off the field. Immediately she was on the telephone again. She called up the doctor who had tended Lou. He reassured her that it had been a minor concussion. But she remained on tenterhooks until at last Lou himself was home again and she could see, hear, and touch him.

The only games to which Eleanor ever invited friends to see Lou — her star husband spoiled the day. The first was a game in Chicago in 1933 where Lou was playing a bang-up game until an easy foul fly was hit in his direction.

'I felt pretty red around the ears,' Eleanor said later, 'when he dropped it.'

The other occasion was the All-Star game in 1934.

On that occasion Lou was one of five American Leaguers that King Carl Hubbell fanned in succession.

On the day Lou finished his sixteen hundredth successive game, Eleanor had a surprise for him. Together with a friend of the family, Fred Fisher, she had finished a baseball song — the first baseball song to be written since the swingy 'Take Me Out to the Ball Game' in 1910.

This time it was a minor, torchy job rather than a rollicking ditty. It never had any particularly spectacular sale.

Mrs. Gehrig always claimed that Lou was responsible for the song.

'I think he's a genius on the ball-field,' she said. 'He thinks I'm a genius at the piano. So I have to prove it, don't I?' The main worry of the song's composition was the fact that it described the agonies of a lad who felt that he couldn't get any place with his girl.

'Everybody knows that Lou and I are happily married,' said Eleanor, 'and I don't want to give them a contrary impression. I'm sure Lou won't take it the wrong way. But just to make sure about it, Mr. Fisher and I have carpentered the lyrics so as to take out all personal feeling.'

In the ensuing years, Eleanor found her job cut out. Lou had never been very quick about money. He had learned to save from his mother, Christina, but he had not learned to talk up for himself or to publicize himself as a player.

Eleanor began to change all that. She dressed him more nattily, she pushed him gently to the fore in social gatherings when she could. She put her business experience in Chicago to work and was responsible in large measure for his salary boosts.

She was his best defender. Once, when Lou was in training camp, a fiery column came out in the *Morning Sentinel* of Orlando, Florida. It was by a guest columnist, Vincent Flaherty, then with the *Washington Times Herald.*

'I'm not in St. Petersburg to praise Gehrig, I'm here to bury the bloke,' it started off. It proceeded to tie into the figure of Lou as a ballplayer and concluded:

> When Gehrig goes it'll mean just the end of another outstanding ballplayer as far as I'm concerned. He was a great team player, a tremendous hitter, but never a great first-baseman. When he leaves I'll be watching the passing of one of the vainest men the game has ever known.... When Gehrig goes, I'll be sitting in on the requiem of a selfish, surly tightwad who milked the game of everything he could and who walked through his career filled with the self-sufficient philosophy that the world owed Gehrig everything.

Sports writers the country over rose to defend Gehrig's honor. But the best defense came from his wife.

Eleanor read it and stood with clenched fists, tears stinging her eyes, tears that soon dried with anger.

'He could never have known Lou at all,' she said. 'Never. The person he is talking about was never any part of Lou.' Which covered the subject completely as far as most people were concerned.

The life of the Gehrigs went along, during those six years from 1933 to 1939, in a happy murmur. They had decided upon their routine and few things disturbed. They had their friends, entertainment, work and hobbies. There was nothing else that mattered.

Then came the bombshell of Lou's retirement in 1939. Eleanor knew how much that streak of games meant to Lou's plugging German nature that wanted to keep on going forever. She knew just the extent of the cruelty that chance had worked on her husband in the prime of his playing years.

Like Lou, she refused bravely to give up any part of their dreams.

In their spacious apartment at Larchmont, New York, Eleanor pointed out the chances Lou had to come back.

'After all, Jimmy Foxx of the Red Sox had a bad year last year — and look how he came out of it,' she declared. She told just how Lou had arrived at the decision.

'He came to me,' Eleanor said, 'and said he thought he would sit down on the bench at last. I didn't know what to say. I knew he hadn't been doing well, but I never thought that it was anything as serious as that — benching himself. We talked it over, mulling it over all day. It was a heartache, that decision. But when he left for Detroit that night, his mind was made up.'

According to Eleanor, there was nothing definite said about it — but each knew how the other stood. Eleanor knew that once Lou's mind was made up his decision was irrevocable; and he knew in turn that his wife would be back of him no matter which way he turned.

'Lou was afraid that Ed Barrow and Joe McCarthy would want to suggest a couple of days off,' she declared. 'Lou didn't want that. He wanted to be the one to do it. I — I was terribly proud when word came through that he had done what I knew he'd do. He did a darned honorable thing.'

The idea of Lou stepping down had first come up back in March when the sports writers were all — except a loyal few— pointing out that Lou had slowed up and was about ready to retire, honorably.

'You've been around first base so long,' Eleanor said, smiling, 'that you might think you have a permanent lease there now.'

Lou knew he was bad, but he hoped that the kinks would iron themselves out as they had in other years. When they didn't, he was reconciled to getting off the first sack. It was no flash decision, as Eleanor knew. She knew that Lou would stay in as long as he thought the Yankees would benefit by his being there. The early sports-writer cries of 'beer legs' and 'muscle-bound' had never bothered him. Nor did they now.

'When he started out,' said Eleanor Gehrig proudly, 'Miller Huggins advised him to hustle and save. He has always done both ever since. Lou has no delusions of grandeur, no false pride. He quit when he decided to quit.'

But both of them thought it was temporary. Neither of them had a thought of the consequences when Eleanor suggested casually one morning:

'Why don't you go out to the Mayo Clinic, Lou? They might help you.'

And when that fatal news came back, they were still unshaken. Lou stood, white with an uncertain grin on his face, his arm about Eleanor's shoulders. She gripped him tighter and said:

'Whatever this is, we'll see it through together.'

She knew that baseball had been more than Lou's job. It had been his whole life. And Eleanor knew too, that Lou had been more than a job of love to her. He was her life from now on.

The old days were gone. No more waiting at the fireside while her famous husband struck out or smashed a home run. No more agony over his being

called a bum, over his being hurt, no more pride in
his achievements. Eleanor once thought that such a
condition would be heaven, but now she knew differ-
ently.

Little things manifested themselves. Once, if Lou
was in a slump or had a bad day at bat, he would
drive home from the Stadium like a madman, hitting
eighty miles an hour or more, sometimes getting
stopped by a motor-cycle policeman but always
being waved on with, 'Oh, it's you, Lou.'

Now Lou, his face still smiling but with tell-tale
lines upon it, was content to drive home at the ordinary citizen's pace of thirty-five miles an hour.

For a player who was once of the 'Spit-tobacco-on-
it-and-it'll-be-all-right' school to be so suddenly removed from the sphere of play, Lou's retirement was
a doubly hard blow. He spent hours by the radio
listening to the Yankee games, his scrapbook at his
feet, fondling his most cherished memento of baseball
— a polished hickory bat with a slight bluish stain
near one end. It was the bat that had crashed a home
run into the bleachers from the pitch of the great
Dizzy Dean in the All-Star game in 1937.

Through all this Eleanor kept herself in the rôle
of the unobtrusive helpmate. She had her job cut out.
She had to make Lou rest whenever he was tired —
instantly. She fed him milk and meat and made him
eat them until he was stuffed and got back the poundage he had lost in the first months of his inactivity.

It was Eleanor's job, too, to fulfill Lou's quiet injunction:

'Please ask all my friends not to make a fuss over me!'

Lou never knew that Eleanor had been on the verge of hysteria for two days. It seemed, she said, 'so unfair that he should be stricken when he had lived so cleanly.' But she pulled herself together, they talked things out, heart-to-heart, for a day and a half and the Gehrig household rode on a resolutely even keel.

Eleanor knew his interests. She knew that they would find mutual comfort in following baseball, in reading, in going to grand opera and the theater, in traveling.

'We've had a shock,' she told reporters. 'But we're not going to ever let it lick us. We're not going to let it change our life any more than we can help. We can't plan far ahead, but I'm going to believe that he will get better and to remember that medicine keeps making new discoveries all the time.'

Eleanor lowered her voice, for Lou was in the next room and she didn't want him to know that she was dramatizing him — a thing he hated above all others.

'And I never admired my husband as much as I do now for the way he's taking the whole thing,' she whispered. 'It's queer how you can live with a person for years and not know how fine they are. I know Lou — now.'

❦

Tarzan Lou

THE baseball season of 1934 was not a notable one for Lou in any single respect. But such was his all-round excellence that there is little doubt that the year after his marriage brought him the full flower of his ability to play ball and the corresponding rewards.

For the first time Lou won the batting title of the league, snapping it away from under the nose of Charlie Gehringer, stellar second-baseman. He had done better than .363 three previous times, but in 1934 this was the top mark. He also smashed four home runs with the bases full. This was the fourth regular season that he had done it and it equaled a major-league record. In 1934, too, Lou again led the runs-batted-in column with 165. Some of his longevity records began to come home to roost. He had knocked out 409 bases on his 210 hits that year, making it the fourth season he went above the 400 mark, breaking a tie with Chuck Klein. That season also was the eighth season where Lou had hit above .300.

But the one record that touched Lou where he lived was the home-run record. Lou hit 49 round trips. The Babe was fading, and he only played in 125 games and knocked out 22 home runs.

Lou was also selected to play on the American League team in the All-Star game and was later given a place on the All-Star team of both leagues — the fourth time he had been awarded that honor.

But in spite of the fact that Lou had had his best all-round year, the Yankees, who had finished second in 1933, also finished second in 1934 to the Detroit Tigers.

This was a hangover from the season of 1933, where the Yanks had made a spurt-start by winning their first eleven games and then falling behind the Washington Senators. Except momentarily in July, Washington held the lead all the way in to the finish. During 1933, Lou had hit only thirty-two home runs, his poorest season since 1928 in that department, and his average at bat dropped to .334.

Lou set to work to find out what had happened to his hitting — always his main worry — and found he was not stepping into the ball as he had been heretofore. This was remedied — and the results showed in the 1934 season. Then, too, a worry had been removed. Lou no longer had to worry about breaking

Everett Scott's 1307-game streak. Lou had passed that with almost more than fifty games to spare. He had ended the 1933 season with 1360 games put away on the books.

About this time, Lou, with Eleanor, went on a world tour, including a barnstorming trip with the Babe and the rest of the players. Lou brought back a lot of sprightly anecdotes and a glittering wardrobe that he would show to any visitor to his home at the drop of a haberdasher's pin.

'Look at this,' he would boom, opening the closet door. Inside would be his major exhibits of Japanese pajamas and kimonos; his prized Piccadilly neckties, aglow properly upon a rack; and on the shelf his long-deserted golf sticks ranged in neat rows.

'Put me off my ball game,' says Lou. 'I don't fool with it now — but wait!'

The main dish in his wardrobe, however, was his famous collection of four suits — two blues, a gray, and a brown — made on Saville Row by the tailor of the Prince of Wales — now Duke of Windsor. Lou always wore them when he could. Conservative in cut, they were the perfect fit to show off his enormous shoulders.

Lou's favorite story about the trip was how he paid five dollars to see a cobra-mongoose fight in Bombay.

'I was fishing around for the right Indian coins to make five dollars,' he said, 'when I heard a tootle-toot and a guy in a turban with a trick musical horn passed right in front of me followed by mister mongoose. Things like that at close range always give me the creeps and I jumped back. When I did I dropped several Straits Settlement dollars which I had been keeping for souvenirs.

'I never got a chance to get them back. The fight got along then and there and I guess some kids ran off with them. Anyway, the fight was no bargain. The bushy-tailed little mongoose beat the cobra to the punch, gripping it by the neck and shaking it. The mongoose shook and shook and the snake died. That's all there was to it, except that it was a little messy.'

In the spring of 1934, too, Lou got his chance to put in a good word for fishing. This was always his favorite sport, and he was forever dragging Eleanor out into the woods on expeditions and going out on Long Island Sound to get soaked during a day's fishing.

In March, he and Eleanor went down to the Long Key, Florida, Fishing Camp, and there Lou caught his first sailfish.

'I don't think there's any thrill in the world like catching a sailfish,' said Lou, who had known more thrills in his life than most people dream of. He proceeded to write his feelings up for the newspapers.

Right after lunch, just when I was beginning to think

that we wouldn't get a chance to get a sailfish, I felt the peculiar tap that tells you a sail is striking at your bait with his bill.... When he had it I set the hook and the battle was started.

The sailfish doubtless didn't know that persistent Lou was on the other end of the line or it wouldn't have started the whole business.

The fish at once leaped clear of the water, with his big blue sail set, his long silvery body shimmering, and his head shaking back and forth trying to release the hook. He went down and made two more leaps. Then he came halfway back to the boat while I reeled in. Then he made another long run, deep down ... I thought I had lost him.

His next maneuver was to rise out of the water and 'walk,' as anglers call it, on the surface for about fifty feet. That gave me the greatest thrill of all.... But it didn't do this fellow any good and after a few more jumps and runs, we had him in the boat.

When the 1935 season opened, Lou looked woefully inept. He was not hitting at all. His average for the exhibition circuit (on which he never hit well) was .069. A traveling friend heard of his slump and sent him a playful wire from Russia: 'Will be glad to rush you slow-motion pictures of my incomparable batting style.'

Babe Ruth had gone, and many of the Yanks were aging as baseball years go. The slow Yankee start was laid by some to the fact that the Oriental tour had slowed them up. A ban against barnstorming trips was talked of and passed. Lou agreed, inasmuch as it applied to major-leaguers playing with bush teams, but said that foreign tours should be continued.

'Good-will tours are great,' he declared. 'My understanding of the rule is that it would permit such an expedition in the future if the league saw fit to send up a real big-league aggregation handled in a big-league way.'

The accusation was repeated later that the twenty-seven games abroad had tired Lou out — especially as he made a slow start. Lou lost no time in refuting that.

'It's about time I said something and ended all these pipe dreams,' he exclaimed. 'It's true I couldn't hit the size of my hat in the early days of the season. But I made up for it.'

The figures show that he did. On May 29, Lou was hitting .238. By September 29 he had finished the season with an average of .329.

But the Yanks ended up in second place for the third year. McCarthy, it was rumored, was building a new team around Lou. Lou himself had finished off the season by batting in over a hundred runs for the tenth time, and had walked five times in succession in a game in August as a tip to the way pitchers thought of him. That same month on the eighth, he had played his 1600th game and celebrated it by hitting his 366th home run.

More honor than that had come to Lou, however. For the first time since 1922, the Yankees had a captain and his name was Lou Gehrig. The last captain had been Babe Ruth. The Babe had been removed from the post by order of Ban Johnson, then president of the American League. The immediate reason for Babe's deposition was the fact that he had chased a baseball fan who had yelled uncomplimentary names at him. The chase lasted quite some time and ranged through most of the Stadium. There was also a fine of fifty dollars.

At the time it was felt that Johnson's action was not entirely without prompting from Miller Huggins and Ed Barrow. The Babe had been overlapping his duties as captain into the manager's province for some time.

With the appointment of Lou, it was felt that at last the Yanks had a man who was level-headed and whose retiring ways would not cause embarrassment to any of the higher-ups. With the passing of the Babe, as well, Lou with his thirty-one thousand dollars salary was now the highest-priced player in the major leagues, as well as the most honored. McCarthy, in naming him for the appointment, also dubbed him the 'greatest.'

Lou told Grantland Rice his philosophy at this juncture in his career, the homespun stuff that he had built his life on. In an interview, Lou said soberly:

'You've got to have a certain philosophy in this world to face some of the bumps or you'll be in for a rough time. I still say that the fellow who keeps himself in shape, who refuses to be discouraged by the bad breaks, who keeps on hustling with the best he had, should make the grade... it's the general average that counts, not a big day or a bad day.'

In 1936, the glory that was the Yankees returned again. Lou, who was one of the leaders on the 1927 team which was now being compared to the 1936 aggregation, was still a stalwart and still amassing honors for himself. When the Yanks steam-rollered all opposition and won the pennant by a record margin, Lou was the recipient of most of the record honors.

Early in the season he had been given a testimonial dinner at the Biltmore in New York. Two huge eight-foot bats, each weighing thirty-five pounds and bearing the names of 1504 sandlot players on them — a number equal to the number of games Lou had played in successively up to that time — was etched upon them.

Lou lived up to this expression of faith in his ability. Again he hit forty-nine home runs to tie his own mark of two years before, and lead the league. He ran his string to 1818 games. He scored over one hundred runs for the eleventh straight season, for the fifth time he totaled more than four hundred bases. For the sixth time he drove in over a hundred and fifty runs.

He also took part in one of his first publicity stunts since his early days in baseball. Under the auspices of the New York *Journal-American*, he tossed a 1935 silver dollar across the Harlem River at 161st Street. Cocking his famous left arm before suitable witnesses, Lou hurled the coin about 460 feet to a snow-covered dock, through a smoke screen from a passing tug. It was hailed as quite a feat, comparing with that of George Washington's fling over the Rappahannock River. That stream is now only 229 feet wide, but in Washington's day it was supposed to be 1320 feet wide.

Not even this stunt — which baseball players say would have jinxed any other team — put the kibosh on the Yankees. By the end of 1936 the team had thirty-one records — either broken or tied. They led the American League to its greatest year in which the other teams turned in twenty-four performances which made major-league history and thirteen which tied old baseball marks. In addition, twenty-four of its own standards were bettered and eleven were tied. Seven new records were put down in individual club books, and ten World Series marks were beaten, seven tied, and for the six-game series seven were topped and three were tied.

In the World Series the Yankees kept up their

sweep. They set seventeen and tied ten World Series records.

In the series against the Giants — their bitterest rivals in those days — the Yankees won, four games to two. Lou put the fourth game, generally conceded to be the turning point, on ice by cracking a home run off Hubbell with a man on base.

The season was over and Lou was the acknowledged head of all baseball players. He had at last achieved the spotlight where the Babe had so often paraded.

But just as the season ended, there came a sudden change in the sporting halo surrounding Lou. The atmosphere changed from hero-worship to a healthy humor.

Suddenly, like a Klieg light from the blue, Lou got the yen for Hollywood.

Nobody knew how. Nobody knew when. But suddenly, there it was.

The first thing the public knew, Christy Walsh, Lou's part-time manager, was making an announcement that Lou would try out for the vacated Tarzan rôle in the movies. The previous occupant of the rôle had been Johnny Weismueller, but now the studio was looking for a new body.

Christy had heard that a new series, sans Weismuller, was on the way. So he wired the West Coast. Back came the reply: 'Are interested in Gehrig. Send pix of him in something besides flannel baseball suit.'

Christy got Lou to strip and pose in a leopard skin. And as Lou stood there, dead-pan, with his bull-neck and piano-legs protruding from the leopard skin, he explained his position to the sports writers.

'It may sound screwy to you guys,' said Lou, 'but I'm dead serious. I'll emote like anything, all over the place — if I get the right dough. I've always been too busy with athletics to test my acting ability, but I've got radio and vaudeville experience. Don't worry, it won't interfere with my playing. I'll be back with the Yanks in the spring.'

Eleanor, at his side, said she had no objection.

'Irene Dunne and Ginger Rogers are plenty of competition, but there's no objection from this end as long as Lou brings home that pay check,' she said.

Lou, however, got a little worried about the production end.

'Maybe they'll have an ape slinging coconuts at me and I'll be bashing back at them with a war-club,' he said musingly. 'I dunno.'

So the wires hummed merrily between New York and Hollywood and the chief topic was Lou's adaptability for the rôle. Lou joined in the whole thing with gusto.

'I've started right in to eat raw meat for the rôle,' he told reporters. 'No more of this pickled-eel phony stuff for me. Wait until you see my butcher bill.'

Then his expression changed. He hitched his chair

forward. 'On the level, fellows,' he said, 'this is a swell idea. It'll be a vacation for me and the missus, a good way to spend the off-season. What better way than making money?'

Christy Walsh told the press that everything was set for final negotiations and that Sol Lesser, of Principal Productions, was keeping Lou on the fire. 'I've handled Lou for several reasons,' he said, 'and this is all part of the job.'

'After all,' said Christy, 'what better Tarzan? Here is Lou, six feet one, two hundred and ten pounds in condition, thirty-four-inch waist, forty-seven-inch chest, and a pair of shoulders that would hardly fit on the screen. Why not a war-club instead of a thirty-six-ounce bat?'

So rumors flew. Then, as suddenly as the tempest of publicity had arisen, it simmered down to nothing. Everything was quiet on the West Coast front for the winter of 1936–37.

In the spring, the lid blew off again. The first announcement came March 3, this time from Hollywood. Lou had arrived out there, somewhat under cover, and signed a one-movie contract.

'I won't go for any of this Tarzan stuff, either,' said Lou decisively. Evidently the kidding that some of his fellow ballplayers had been giving him had been getting under his skin.

'I hope to do something for the screen,' said Lou

dreamily. 'I hope they can — er — do something for me, too.'

In his first unscheduled appearance on the silver screen — which was at the airport before newsreel cameramen — Lou didn't do so well. They gave him his lines, but Lou muffed them.

'Struck out,' he grinned. 'Throw me another.' They did and everything went off in record time. Lou lost no time in saying that he had no intention of infringing on his baseball career.

Although Lou himself had denied that he would play Tarzan, his first tests were for that rôle. But Lessar, observing Lou's knobby knees and spike-scarred ankles, turned thumbs down. He decided on another picture which his scenarists whipped up.

This script was titled 'Rawhide,' and in it Lou would wear pants. It was the story of a rustler-manglin', straight-shootin' cowboy who rides down into Pleasant Valley and rids the place of all the rustler varmints and makes it a fitten place for God and man to live in again.

Lou objected. 'I'm not so good on a horse,' he said. 'And I'm not so good with pistols.'

'Shootin'-irons,' corrected a scenarist.

'I'm still not so good,' said Lou stubbornly. Then he pointed out, too, that he couldn't sing a lick and that most cowboy heroes had to yodel their heads off through a picture. Lastly, said Lou uneasily, he would probably have to make love to some blonde he had never seen before. They reassured him on the last point; it's a rule that cowboy heroes never kiss the heroines.

So production started. The script was revised somewhat so that Lou played the rôle of Lou Gehrig who has retired from the diamond and bought a ranch only to find it infested with rustlers. He runs them down, shoots them one by one, and ends up by getting a call from the Yankees to come back and play.

Lou, cantering gently down the main street of a jerry-built movie town, had the time of his life. Keeping a careful grip on the saddlehorn, and one hand on his six-shooters, he swaggered into the Palace Saloon (imitation) and said in a full Bronx accent:

'Boy, this is more fun than the World Series!'

His main harassment came from the crowds of youngsters who kept massing around him asking for his autograph. Lou genially assented to all requests.

'What I'd like to do,' he said, 'is to make movies in the winter and play ball in the summer.'

Hollywood had an excellent chance to indulge in its inimitable ribbing. The first time Lou climbed on his horse, he found it equipped with a pair of bicycle handlebars. 'My pal, Eleanor, razzed me for a week when she heard I was going to ride,' he said sheepishly. 'But so far I haven't even got a blister.'

Lou refused to make the usual publicity stills with pretty girls. 'None of that,' he said decisively. 'I've got my girl.' He seemed perfectly composed before the camera, outside of the fact that he broke down when a trained penguin wandered across in front of the camera just as a take was being made.

In his trips to and from the West Coast and New Rochelle, where Eleanor was staying, Lou forgot a nightshirt. Christy Walsh found it and scuttled from studio to studio, getting autographs from all the glamour stars such as Jean Harlow, Jeanette MacDonald, Mae West, and the rest. By the end of the day he had twenty-five names on it — all from women. He wrapped it up and sent it air mail to New York and waited for results.

The only result was a staid announcement from the Gehrig home that henceforth Eleanor would accompany Lou on his trips.

About the only harsh note in the whole of the Gehrig Hollywood proceedings came from Edgar Rice Burroughs, author of the Tarzan Series. He saw some tests of Lou as Tarzan and proceeded to wire the Yankee player:

HAVE SEEN SEVERAL PICTURES OF YOU AS TARZAN AND PAID ABOUT FIFTY DOLLARS FOR NEWSPAPER CLIPPINGS ON THE SUBJECT I WANT TO CONGRATULATE YOU ON BEING A SWELL FIRST BASEMAN

The actual making of the picture was a lark for
Lou. It was not nearly so hard and nearly so thrilling
as pounding around the bases. He had never been
on a horse before in his life — nor before a camera —
but everybody assured him that didn't matter.

'Just act natural,' Director Ray Taylor told him.
Lou did. He sauntered about with his ten-gallon hat
on, flapping his chaps, and Taylor watched with a
critical eye. He nodded. 'The big fellow will do,'
was his judgment.

When Lou was told to whip his horse into a gallop,
he applied the quirt apprehensively. The horse
flicked a languid eye backward and broke into what
was later described as a 'lazy lope.' But when Lou
saw the first rushes of the picture the horse was
going like mad.

'I knew it was only a trick of camera speedup,'
Lou said afterward, 'but even in the audience, it
scared me.'

On one occasion he was sitting eating between
members of the cast of 'Rawhide,' watching the
various cowboys and Western bad men with a fasci-
nated gaze. Suddenly Lou gulped. Down at the
other end of the board, two of the most evil-looking
hombres he had ever seen had risen and were in the
midst of a terrific argument, hands on their holsters.

There was a lightning-quick draw. A shot exploded in the narrow room. Lou gasped and jumped
to his feet.

Then he saw the fallen cowboy get up and resume his meal. The others had not stirred, still going on with their champing and munching. Lou realized a little late that it was a gag.

When the picture was finally shown in St. Petersburg, Florida, at the Yankees training camp, the sports writers reviewed it and were very kind.

'Lovely Lou Gehrig is no Gable and perhaps it's just as well,' said one review. 'But he is a definite photogenic type and ... he shows surprising poise and ability in his début before the cameras.'

In the picture Lou's baseball training is the salvation of his ranch. He bounces pool balls off the head of the villain and at one tense moment manages to rescue the situation by fungoing a baseball through a window. He also sung a verse of some forgotten song in a bashful way and in the general opinion — outside team snickers from the Yankees — was 'vastly superior' to a corny opus.

Of course there was the rib to come. When Lou reported for training, Lefty Gomez pretended he was a movie director and gave Lou the 'scream test' perched on chairs in the clubhouse. They gave him two cap pistols and Red Ruffing, the Yank pitcher, offered to be his horse.

'Very good, Mr. Gehrig,' intoned Gomez, 'you and the horse looked fine. Now I want you both to come out shooting. Roll it! Very fine, Mr. Gehrig;

all the bad bandits are dead, thanks to you. That is all.'

The final note on the picture, oddly enough, came from Pittsfield, Massachusetts. Two customers there demanded their money back at a showing on the 'Great Garrick,' a costume picture starring Brian Aherne. They said they had gone in under the impression that the picture was starring Lou.

Lou was a week late at the training camp. He had been a holdout for a salary raise and both he and Colonel Ruppert — to whom he had gone personally for the first time — had been obdurate. There had been some fairly bitter words between the two, with Lou holding out for fifty thousand dollars and the Colonel rasping, 'See you in the movies, Lou,' but finally it was settled amicably. The final price was the Colonel's — thirty-nine thousand dollars.

It was the highest price Lou ever got, but it was still way off the Babe's pace of eighty thousand dollars.

In the season of 1937, Lou kept right on going. He passed the 1900-game mark on August 3. That event he celebrated by knocking out a home run in a Yankee double-header and George M. Cohan presented him with a gold watch between games on Lou Gehrig Appreciation Day.

Lou followed through by getting the 2500th hit of his career and then on August 31, he hit a home run with the bases filled — the twenty-second time he had succeeded in such a feat. The Yankees went on to win the pennant, Lou to his sixth — and last — appointment to the All-Star team. The Giants won the National League pennant and faced the Yankees with fear and trembling, to lose, four games to one.

At the end of this season, Tony Lazzeri was released. He was the last of the Old Gang. Now there was only Lou Gehrig and his constant friend and room-mate, Bill Dickey, remaining of the crowd that had made baseball history under the tutelage of Miller Huggins.

It was apparent that Lou was slipping. In 1937 he had had sixteen major errors to become high man among the A-1 first basemen. His hitting, of course, had been up to par, at .351, but there seemed to be some of the sparkle missing from his play.

But none of his persistence or thoroughness was missing. He and Eleanor had shopped all over New York for Christmas cards the Christmas before. They had found none which suited them. So it was decided that they would write personal letters — half of them by Mrs. Gehrig, half by Lou. It was a tough job, but it was put through and neither one got writer's cramp.

And Lou still was as contemptuous as ever of physical injury. He had an injured finger, swollen

and sore with a ligament torn, but he was still batting
.360. It interfered a little with his throwing, but that
was all.

The season of 1938 saw his first decline. A short
survey of his first few weeks with the team illustrates
how badly Lou had fallen off.

Boston, April 18: Yanks drop opener to Red Sox. Gehrig
hitless.

Boston, April 19: Yanks win one; lose one. Gehrig hitless in
seven times at bat.

Boston, April 21: Yanks lose. Gehrig hitless in five times.
Fourteen hitless attempts in four games. Consecutive
game 1969.

New York, April 22: Defeat Washington. Gehrig at bat three
times; no hits.

New York, April 23: Washington wins. Gehrig gets first hit
of season. After seventeen attempts without a bingle, he
smacked a lusty double. So tickled, Lou tried to stretch
the drive, a blast of 407 feet off the right center bleacher
wall, into a triple. He missed by a stride at third base.
Afterward he hit into a double play, walked, flied out, and
walked.

New York, April 24: Yanks win from Washington. Gehrig
hitless in three times.

Philadelphia, April 25: Yanks lose. Gehrig: no hits, three
walks in four times up.

Philadelphia, April 26: Yanks win. Gehrig gets a double and
bats in Rolfe in three times at plate. Hit brings total to two.

Philadelphia, April 27: Yanks win. They call him Double-
or-Nothing Lou now. Knocked another two-bagger for his
third hit of the season. At plate four times. Gehrig still in
clean-up position.

New York, April 28: Yanks lose to Red Sox. Three times up
and no hits. Batting average: .088.

New York, April 29: Yanks beat Sox at Stadium's first

Ladies' Day. Responding to shrieks, Gehrig hit two singles for his first two-hit game, and brought his total to five hits. He scored from first when he ran home on Dickey's double. Knocked in his third run of the year. His 1977th game. Heard for the first time the old cry of 'We want a homer.'

April 29: Gehrig is at the bottom of the average column.

Games	AB	R	H	HR	RBI	SB	Av.
12	38	7	5	0	3	0	.132

Washington, April 30: Yanks win. Gehrig hitless in five times at plate.

Washington, May 1: Yanks lose. Gehrig hitless in three times up.

Washington, May 2: Yanks win. Gehrig gets first hit in eleven trips to plate in last four games, a single. At bat three times. Gehrig moved to six position and Di Maggio, who has been hitting lustily, gets clean-up spot. Gehrig's 1980th successive game.

New York, May 3: Yanks beat Browns. Gehrig gets his first homer in the first inning. It was inside the park, bounding out to the 461-foot corner of center field near the monument to the late Miller Huggins. Ball escaped Sammy West and Gehrig beat throw at plate by a step. Lou also hit a double and knocked in two runs in three trips to the plate.

New York, May 4: Yanks win. No hits for Gehrig, in three times at bat.

New York, May 5: Yanks win. Gehrig gets single and double in five trips to plate.

May 5: Gehrig still at the bottom of American League Average column.

Games	AB	R	H	HR	RBI	SB	Av.
18	59	10	10	1	5	0	.169

New York, May 7: Yanks beat Tigers. Gehrig gets his first triple, and two singles, to knock in two runs. Five times at bat.

New York, May 8: Defeat White Sox. Lou's 1985th game found him leading the way. Parked a homer in the right-field stand (note: first time he's found right-field stand this year), later hit a single. AB: 4; R: 2; H: 2.

New York, May 11: Yanks take lead, beating Indians for seven straight games. Gehrig: four times at bat; one single.

New York, May 12: Feller beats Yanks. Gehrig hit third homer of the season into right-field stands for two runs. Also made a single. Two in four. Average: .237.

Something was radically wrong. This was not the Lou Gehrig that the baseball world had known. He ended up the year with a batting average below .300 — .295 — for the first time in thirteen years. He broke eight records to lead the league, but most of them were his own already and were longevity records anyway.

Something was wrong. This was neither ball-player Lou nor Professor Gehrig of Columbia who the year before had stood up on the platform and said:

'The way to hit is to step into it.'

Players agreed that somehow Lou had become ball-shy. There was no explanation for it. The hero was still there, bulky and as good-humored as ever, though puzzled. The kids still gathered around for autographs. They did not know that two years later their hero would be lying on a bed and would have to ask a nurse to direct his hand to autograph an old score-card for an Illinois fan.

But Lou turned up as usual in 1939 for the practice

sessions of the Yanks, grimly determined to make himself succeed. He drove himself around the track and batted balls into the air. His only thought was to get himself into condition. Then, he was convinced, everything would come back with a rush.

'These big guys,' said Ty Cobb, watching him, 'they go fast. When they fall apart, it's like the one-hoss shay.'

In his determination to make good, Lou had taken a pay cut of four thousand dollars. And as a reward, although his spring training session had been miserable, he started with the team as usual. His head was high over the whispers of his team-mates, the rumors printed in the newspapers. Lou had fought his own battle with Eleanor by his side and his mind was at peace.

McCarthy, quizzed by the reporters, repeated his statement of the old halcyon days: 'The kid stays in until he takes himself out.' Yet he knew that Lou couldn't run, hit, or field properly; that he was miserable at the swift decline that had come upon him.

Joe only knew that Lou must work his problem out for himself. And he let time take its course.

Lou struggled through the first eight games of the season. He made four hits. His average at bat was .143.

But it was not that consideration that brought him to the final crossroads of decision. The last game he played was on April 30 at the Yankee Stadium. He made the last put-out of the game, taking a throw from Johnny Murphy, the pitcher.

Lou had a hard time bending to get the ball. A gigantic hand of pain seemed to grip him in the back. But he got it and ran heavily and wearily back to the first sack.

When the play was over and the players were jogging toward the clubhouse, Murphy ran over to Lou.

'Lou,' he said, putting his arm around the big fellow's shoulders. 'That was a nice play, Lou.'

Then Lou knew the worst. He knew that the play had been the essence of simplicity. He knew that a tyro could have done it better, that only the stellar play of Joe Gordon at the second sack had made it possible for him to stay on the Yankee team at all.

Best of all, Lou knew his decision.

'I knew I was washed up,' he said.

Lucky Lou

IT HAPPENED in Detroit. It was May 2, 1939, a warm sunny day, perfect baseball weather.

Manager Joe McCarthy had just flown in from Buffalo, where he was looking over some Yankee prospects. When he came into the hotel lobby with his quick, nervous stride, Lou Gehrig came up to him. It was the way he had cornered Miller Huggins once to ask him for a playing job. Now it was for a different purpose.

'Joe,' said Lou. 'I'd like to talk to you.'

He was his quiet, reserved self. He had a grin but that was all. His eyes were serious. His face was pale under its tan, his great figure seemed wilted in the blue pin-stripe suit.

Joe McCarthy glanced sharply at Lou.

'Sure,' he said. 'Come around the corner here and sit down.'

He knew what was coming. A long time ago, when the fans were clamoring for Lou to be taken out — for his own good as well as the team's — McCarthy had said his say:

'The big fellow plays just as long as he wants to play.'

But now Joe knew.

There was a light sweat on Lou's forehead. Without preamble, directly, as he always talked, Lou said what was on his mind.

'Joe,' he began, 'I'm terrible. I'm not helping the team at all. This string of games I've run up really doesn't mean anything. And it isn't fair to the other boys in there for me to stay on at first base. I want you to take me out.'

Joe nodded. He tried to say something, but the lump in his throat came between the words and choked him. He patted Lou on his massive shoulder instead and went upstairs.

That afternoon at the ball park, Lou, as captain of the Yankee team, walked soberly up to the umpire with the batting order. The umpire, with the mask of office in his hand, glanced perfunctorily over the list. Suddenly he stopped. He looked more closely as if he could not believe his eyes.

'Dahlgren, first base,' he read aloud. 'Hey, what's this, Lou?'

He looked up. Tears were streaming down Lou's

cheeks. The umpire gulped and hastily donned his mask. Lou turned slowly and went back to the Yankee bench.

'So,' wrote John Kieran, 'ended an epic.'

So it did. The Iron Horse was derailed, old Biscuit-Pants was no longer on first, the Durable Dutchman was no more. The greatest career of impregnable play in organized baseball had finally come to an end and with it an era — the era of the great days of the Yankees. They were legend and legion now, with the Babe gone, Gehrig out. They were stuff for the old gaffers to chew on, to say I-knew-them-when about.

Lou left a citadel behind him, fortified with records, buttressed with evidences of his power at bat. He had played 2130 games in succession (nearly sixty more, if World Series games are counted); he had hit an average of .340 in those games, no matter his condition or handicaps. He had batted in the unbelievable total of more than 2000 runs (including World Series games). He had batted in 100 runs or more every season from 1926 through 1938. In 1931 he had made 2200 put-outs with less than 200 errors, a fielding average — for the once-clumsy 'Tanglefoot' — of 99 per cent accuracy. He had scored, himself, nearly 2000 runs and had thus accounted for 4000 runs for the Yankees — the only big league team he ever played for — during his fourteen years of play. Thus he had made up more than a third of the Yankees' total punch. An ordinary major-league club scores only 800 runs per season.

This imposing pile — and more — of records left on the books, thought the fans, must have been made by a superman. Yet Lou had declined visibly and with him the Yanks, always a one-man team. As the Babe had gone so the Yanks went. These last few years it had been as their bellwether, Lou, went. And Lou made only four hits in eight games, had slowed down to a .143 batting average, last on the team, as the Yanks sank lower and lower in league standing, fifth in the percentages, last in their once-mighty batting.

What was the reason, the fans wondered?

They did not have long to wait for an answer. Lou Gehrig left New York, himself puzzled by his decline and fall, despondent over his lassitude and lack of pep. He went to the famous Mayo Clinic at Rochester, Minnesota, long the haven of ailing ballplayers.

When he returned, on June 21, 1939, Lou, pale-faced and grim, went directly to the Yankee Stadium and the offices of President Ed Barrow, one of his closest friends. That same day Barrow, white-faced as Lou himself, called in the reporters. Silently he handed them slips of paper. Each one was the same.

This is to certify that Mr. Lou Gehrig has been under examination at the Mayo Clinic from June 13 to June 19, 1939, inclusive.

After a careful and complete examination, it was found that he is suffering from amyotrophic lateral sclerosis. This type of illness involves the motor pathways and cells of the central nervous system and, in lay terms, is known as a form of chronic poliomyelitis — infantile paralysis.

The nature of this trouble makes it such that Mr. Gehrig will be unable to continue his active participation as a baseball player, inasmuch as it is advisable that he conserve his muscular energy. He could, however, continue in some executive capacity.

The release was signed by Harold C. Habein, M.D., of the Clinical Section of the Mayo Clinic.

What the highbrow medical terms meant was this. An eighteen-inch, ounce-heavy section of bone and nerve tissue, the spinal cord, was hardening.

This, said the doctors, was non-infectious, caused by a sub-microscopic virus, and became evident when the muscles, usually in the right hand, began to tighten up and weaken. Then, they said, laughter is uncontrollable. Feet shuffle. Lips flutter and there is difficulty in swallowing. Flesh wastes away and finally the afflicted ones die, veritable skeletons. There is no pain, merely a gradual fading away until death.

There is no recorded case where anyone so diseased has ever perfectly recovered — or indeed, lived at all.

Lou, who had received the fatal news on his thirty-sixth birthday, refused to believe that his case was so bad. He still maintained that calm attitude of mind which had prevailed just after the last game. In that

game he had been at bat four times. He had flied out
three times, grounded out once. His last fly, a tower-
ing hit to center field, might have been a home run
if it had been pulled a bit to right field. But it was,
on any count, his best clout of the season. So Lou
posed for pictures and told the reporters,

'I made up my mind ... I knew it wasn't fair to
the boys, to Joe, to the baseball public, and to myself
to stay in there. It got to be plenty tough walking up
to the plate with winning runs on base and leaving
them there. Joe has been perfectly swell about it all.
He would have left me in there until the cows came
home, I guess, but it wasn't doing any good.'

He remembered the farewell cheers of the crowd
when they heard his decision over the microphone.
He still was captain of the Yankees and could sit on
the bench. He recalled how his team-mates had gone
out and walloped the Detroit Tigers 22 to 2 that same
day, and how they had taken an upward spurt of
spectacular proportions when Babe Dahlgren came
and perched on first base.

Lou always believed that he would come back
again. He felt in his heart that in a little time he
would don the cross-lettered cap of the Yankees and
the uniform and go in again and hit for the fences
with the crowd's swelling acclaim in his ears.

But he never did. Lou Gehrig was through. The
giant had been topped by an almost invisible bug.

'I'm happy that Lou did it himself,' said Wally Pipp, the first baseman of the Yanks that Lou dethroned and who had witnessed the historic incident.

'It wouldn't seem right for someone else to take Lou out,' agreed Dixie Walker, a former team-mate.

'Looks like the great Yankee dynasty is beginning to crumble,' said Hank Greenberg, who was soon to make his own bid for the home-run crown.

But Hank was wrong. Only Lou was gone, and to many people there was an empty space about first base and in their hearts that could not be filled. But looking at him one would never suspect illness.

'I'm feeling great,' he would say, 'on the level. I feel all right, I don't hurt any place, I sleep well, and my appetite — well, you know I have no trouble with my appetite. The only thing — is that I have to keep quiet. That's kind of hard sometimes.'

He would pause and look over the green, sunlit turf of the Stadium. His eyes would be steady when he looked back again but the first words would waver.

'But I've got to keep quiet. You can only beat this thing by concentration on it one hundred per cent, and that's what I intend to do.'

Lou didn't know that there was no medical treatment for his disease, that his resting was only a means to keep him alive longer.

'I wish I could be out there,' he would say. 'But I guess there's nothing new about that. I suppose a lot

of fellows have wished the same thing after they've
got through.'

If the question of Lou's career being cut short at
thirty-six came up, Lou would look up, mild surprise
in his brown eyes.

'Sure, maybe,' he would say. 'But look, I had
fourteen seasons in the big league and I'm grateful
for those. Not many fellows get as good a break as
that. I've got no kick.'

Lou was still the fellow who had no kick against
anything in his life. He was the big fat kid who had
come up from the crowded streets of Yorkville to be
a national figure and who was content to play second
fiddle to whatever buffets Fortune dealt out to him.
He knew what he had been, what he might have been.

'When I went to Sing Sing to play one day, two or
three voices called "Lou! Lou!" to me. I looked
around and there were some of the kids I used to play
with in the streets of Yorkville. I thought then that
if it hadn't been for some good friends, some luck, and
a big pair of shoulders that I might have been right
in their place.'

Now he was contented, though not satisfied. He
had wanted badly to die in harness.

Honors showered down upon him. Baseball celebrated its centennial at the old stamping-ground of its
founder, Abner Doubleday, at Cooperstown, New
York. Although the Board had decided to make no

additions to the Hall of Fame in 1939, the rule was waived in Lou's case and his bronze statue went up beside that of Ruth. Editorials were written, eulogies were poured out in cold type.

Statisticians figured out that he held more records than anyone next to Ty Cobb and his old rival, Babe Ruth. He received full salary for the year — thirty-five thousand dollars, a thousand-dollar cut from 1938, his highest salaried year. But he voluntarily retired from baseball at the end of the season after the Yanks, with his moral humping in their favor, had won their fourth straight world title by defeating the Cincinnati Reds in four straight World Series games. He joined in the celebration, clad in the conductor's cap and coat. 'Gee,' he said, 'I'm sure glad I'm a member of this ball club.'

Two things, perhaps, affected Gehrig most deeply. One was the action of Ed Barrow, who announced that his number 4, so long familiar on his big back to the Yankee fans, would never again be assigned to any Yankee player, an honor never given even to Ruth's number 3. Barrow added that the locker that Lou always used, one at the end of the row near the window where he had first dressed when he came in to see Miller Huggins years ago, a green, timid, wondering kid, would never be used by anyone else. It would, Barrow promised, stay his forever with his name still on it as he left it. Nor would Lou, as long as he lived, ever be off the Yankee team. His name was placed on the voluntarily retired list.

The other event happened on July 4, 1939. That Independence Day, which since has been known as Lou Gehrig Day to Yankee fans, there was the greatest fête ever given a ballplayer by baseball, that notoriously sentimental sport.

More than sixty thousand fans crowded the stands, decked with flags and bunting. It was a gala doubleheader, but nobody remembered what team the Yanks were playing. All they remembered was the sun bright on the grass, the giant curved shadow of the Stadium across the diamond, the blueness of the sky — and Lou Gehrig.

Far down, like pigmies at the plate, were the players and Mayor Fiorello H. La Guardia, the fiery little head of New York City, Postmaster General James H. Farley, the genial Jim, and all the members of the teams crowded around one figure — the massive bulk of Lou Gehrig.

There was the yellow dust around home plate, the voices extolling Lou's long career, the silverware scattered over the ground, a smoking stand, scrolls, fishing-rods — all from the people who had known Lou so long and loved him so well.

Lou choked. The tears streamed down his face. Their own faces working, Ed Barrow and Sid Mercer, the master of ceremonies, stood on each side of him to ask him to speak. But Lou shook his head. At the last, his emotions and the old shyness of his boyhood had overcome his gratitude and humility. He could not speak, for the life of him, until Joe McCarthy came out.

'Talk to them, Lou,' he said. 'Go ahead. That's an order, Lou. They're all your friends and you can't disappoint them. You wouldn't want to disappoint them, Lou.'

'Knock out one more hit,' urged Ed Barrow. 'You're up, Lou.'

Lou looked at Joe and Ed for a moment, then nodded slowly. He stepped with the little shuffle that had come to characterize his steps in the last few months toward the microphone.

Joe McCarthy took one look and fled hastily to the clubhouse. He sat in his office, his head in his hands, not daring to listen to Lou speaking, too wrought up to hear, afraid to let the crowd see the hard-boiled manager of the Yankees going soft.

But down on the diamond Lou had come up to the microphone. For a moment his eyes took in the whole scene, the vast panorama of baseball that he had been part of so long, the leaving of which seemed like taking part of his body from him. The cheers descended from the stands like a tidal wave, swept over him and broke against the other side of the Stadium. Lou stood still.

The Stadium hushed. There was only the sound of the wind, and then Lou was speaking in a carefully level voice that broke at the end of his sentences:

'They say I've had a bad break,' he began. 'But when the office force and the ground-keepers and even the Giants from across the river whom we'd give our right arm to beat in the World Series — when they remember you, that's something. And when you even have a mother-in-law who takes sides against her own daughter, that's something.'

The crowd laughed, but Lou was mopping the sweat from his forehead.

'And when you have a wonderful father and mother who worked hard to give you an education, that's something. And when you have a wonderful wife who has shown more courage than I ever hope to have, that's really great.'

Lou choked again, then went on to speak of the dead Colonel Jacob Ruppert, Ed Barrow, and everyone he could remember connected with the Yankee organization down to the ground-keepers. Then he went on:

'And when you have spent six years with a great little manager like Miller Huggins and the next nine with the finest and smartest manager in baseball to-day, Joe McCarthy — and when you have the privilege of rooming, eating, playing cards, and knowing one of the greatest fellows that ever lived, Bill Dickey ——'

Gehrig shook his head in dead earnestness at the mention of the Yankee catcher, his best friend.

'I may have been given a bad break but I've an awful lot to live for. With all this, I consider myself the luckiest man on the face of the earth.'

The cheers were hysterical. Paper fluttered down, a broken straw hat. In the stands, people were crying unashamedly.

The Babe, his eyes wet, came out and put his arm around Lou's shoulder in the old familiar gesture.

'Here, kid,' he said, his voice hoarse with emotion, 'take — take ——'

The Babe looked around for something to ease his feelings — 'take this old fishing-rod and go catch all the fish in the damned sea.'

Lou grinned crookedly and went back to the Yankee bench. He carried with him a bronze statuette given him by his fellow-players. On the base was a poem by John Kieran to add the lush touch of sentimentality to the occasion.

So it was with a parade of all the champions of 1927 to the flagpole and back, with the faded championship pennant of 1927 blowing in the breezes that were roving in the upper tiers of the bleachers, with bands playing and crowds cheering. It was with the unassuming hero of it all moving quietly in the midst of the tumult, his eyes turned always either upward in repose or else resting with a smile on the box where sat his wife Eleanor and his beloved Christina and Heinrich.

After that it was only going down, playing until Lou's own grim personal game would be called on account of darkness.

There were anti-climactic events, of course. There was the magnanimous gesture of Mayor La Guardia, offering Lou a job on the Parole Board of New York State at fifty-seven hundred dollars a year for ten years, one of three men — about as much salary or a little less than Lou would have got from a single World Series. Lou, who had saved perhaps two hundred and fifty thousand dollars from his earnings, accepted quietly after first spending three months in intense study of prison systems and parole methods and setting up an office behind the austere gilt name of Henry L. Gehrig. He went to that office every day until the end.

There was the usual horde of stories already beginning to cluster about the legendary figure of Larrupin' Lou, some of them prosy fancy, some of them fact with the edges burnished. But the best of all was one that was told by Quentin Reynolds, who once wrote a yarn in 1935 about Lou for *Collier's*. Returning from England, five years later, where he had seen death and disaster in the Nazi bombing raids and more raw courage in a few weeks than most see in a lifetime, Quentin met an Englishman who told him the story of the Bomb Removal Squad Leader.

He related the story of the man who dug out a huge demolition time bomb that had not yet exploded, how he loaded it on a truck, and, carrying what he knew to be death and destruction behind him, trundled it out to the dump, where he left the great bomb to explode harmlessly.

'He did what he knew someone had to do. He risked his own life to save many others,' the Englishman ended. 'It was magnificent. You, I'll wager, have never seen anything approaching such courage.'

Quentin looked up and nodded his curly head. 'Yes,' he said quietly. 'I have. I knew Lou Gehrig.'

So death crept on, but Lou refused to rust in disuse. Each day he went to the office attended by his courageous wife. He turned down a dozen offers of fancy jobs from night clubs and the stage. He refused any testimonials now. Visitors reported:

'It's pretty bad now. His mind is still good but he can't talk very well. Can't control his lips. They light his cigarettes for him. He shuffles a lot.'

Lou soon lived like a semi-hermit because the friends who were still devoted to him could not bear to see him wasting away. But he still had his wife, Christina and Heinrich, and — his scrapbooks. He played sometimes with his pets — two police dogs. Lou rarely talked of his ailment.

'I guess you have to take the bitter with the sweet,' he said once. 'If this is the finish, I'll take it.' But he rarely let himself get that despondent.

The end came with startling suddenness. For a month Lou had been confined to his home on Delafield Avenue in the Fieldston section of the New York Bronx. He had been losing weight steadily and was now down to two hundred pounds from two hundred and thirty. Then for two weeks he was confined to bed. It was just a little over two weeks until he would have been thirty-eight.

Lou was lying still and white on the bed when he died, still conscious. Around him were Christina and Heinrich, both weeping, with Eleanor, his wife, her eyes full of tears but still, by a heroic effort, keeping herself from weeping. Lou looked at them strangely, as if he did not know them; then a flicker or recognition passed over his face. His grip tightened on Eleanor's hand. He smiled, the twisted ghost of the once-big bashful grin he had given everybody.

Then his body relaxed, bit by bit. He had said nothing. He had died, almost in his sleep.

It was 10.10 P.M., June 2, 1941, exactly sixteen years to the day after Lou had started his record string of big-league games.

Two days later all the flags in New York were at half-mast. The kids playing ball in Central Park, where Lou used to bat them out for them and anger Huggins by doing it, were talking in whispers about their idol's death. In Japan, where Lou had once played, there was sorrow in the Samurai. In the Ba-

hamas a fisherman heard the news on the air and
whispered,'He was the greatest, all right.'

The Babe said, 'I'm sorry, sorry as hell. He was
one of those guys who never quit.'

Lou's body lay in state at a church near his home.
Thousands filed past, truck-drivers and socialites,
grimy urchins and sober business men. They saw the
same man they remembered, a little gray at the
temples, in a blue business suit, the familiar dimples
visible in the faint smile that was on his face.

In Detroit that day the Yanks had stood in Briggs
Stadium, where Lou had ended his own career two
years before, stood in sad silence and lost to the
Tigers, 4 to 2.

All over the sporting world that had known Lou
there was much grief at his death. But there was one
side light that would have pleased Lou, if he had
known it, as perhaps he did, warming up on some
empyrean diamond. Lou had the best of durability,
even in death.

No man, the doctors knew, had ever outlived his
disease, chronic polio, for more than two years. Lou
had beaten that record by a month. Even in death
Lou remained what he had been in life, the Durable
Dutchman.

'I've had no kick,' he always said.

Epilogue

THE fall and decline of Lou Gehrig is a classic catastrophe. He seems more gigantic than ever in the shadows. If, to the oncoming, skeptical generation, his feats seem only ordinary, there are always the elder baseball fans to remind them that there was once a time when giants walked the earth in spiked shoes.

Oddly enough, this magnification of a man into a legend is the thing Lou would have wanted least. He never asked anything of the crowds. He courted neither their favor nor their frowns. He was a baseball journeyman who did his chores exceedingly well. He was fashioned for giving thrills rather than receiving them.

In baseball the crowd is fickle. Popularity, won through years, may be lost in an hour. Appraisal is gimlet-eyed, judgment quick, the forgetting short and final. For those who fail there is only oblivion — the crush of departing fans at the exits, the shower of torn newspapers, the lonely ranks of the bleacher benches.

This may happen to Lou, especially since he denied himself the learning of those tricks which make for the

front pages. But somehow the opposite seems to be
coming true. His very modesty and self-effacement
are working to immortalize him.

Perhaps here is a man who overreaches the limita-
tions of a sport and assumes the stature of a man.
No legend can stand unless its core is real and lasting.
What is there about Lou Gehrig that will make him
last longer than the record books?

Lou was the prototype of the American dream —
straight from the pages of Horatio Alger. During his
fourteen years in big-league organized ball, during his
two years in minor-league bush ball, during his boyhood and schoolhood of playing baseball, he betrayed
none of the earmarks of greatness.

Lou had none of the superhuman attributes of ham-
handed Honus Wagner, greatest of the short-stops.
He had none of the dramatic flair of Babe Ruth, none
of the electric fire of Ty Cobb. Nor did he even have
the smooth perfection of Nap Lajoie, the hitting ability of Sisler, or the fielding talent of Chance.

But he was fortunate enough to be human. His
engaging grin and lack of cockiness, the shy, self-
effacing mannerisms that came naturally to him, his
very real unadaptability to the game which he over-
came by hard work rather than by flashy talent —
all these combined to make him a figure of lovable,
down-to-earth proportions.

Lou was loved by those that knew him for these

things. They admired his solid virtues of reliability and studied efficiency as well. But these did not appear to the fans in the ninety-nine-cent seats. Lou did not have the indefinable gift of making himself beloved by the common man.

'I never heard anybody boo Lou,' one reporter said.

That was not true in the literal sense. When Lou came up to bat, swinging a cluster of three bats over his square shoulders, there was often a shower of boos and Bronx cheers. But these expressions of disparagement were unrelated to his personal effect upon the crowd. They feared what his bludgeon might do to the team they favored. Not a fan among the booers but would have been insulted if anyone had intimated that he held a personal dislike for Lou.

The other greats of baseball have always been universally loved and hated, personally and violently. Because of this, such figures as Cobb and Ruth have risen to legendary heights with their caps with nubbins of chewing gum on the peak in the clouds and their feet still on the diamond. About these, sports writers have woven a thousand stories, and the fans believe them because they choose to believe.

The legend of Lou Gehrig is new to the history of sport — at least in baseball. It derives its vitality from the fact that although this man inspired no passion, he did arouse a lasting affection, even in the hearts of those who only saw him hunched over the plate waiting for the first pitch.

For he reflects what America dreams of being. He rose from the poorest circumstances by his own labor. He carefully avoided any actions that might have brought injury to others. He made himself what he wanted to be and carved a niche in the spot he himself selected.

And, finally, when he had reached the top, he did not forget the long way he had come and the obligations it entailed. Lou made no bones of the debt he owed his mother and his wife. He never failed to pay tribute to Miller Huggins and Joe McCarthy or his team-mates. Although he worked most of his active life in the shadow of the greatest ballplayer that American baseball has ever known, he had no complaint to make — only compliments.

Lou set his own standards. When he reached them, which was rarely, he was satisfied. When he fell short he was fiercely indignant and set about to analyze them, and then work them out by constant practice on the field.

Once or twice, as if to prove his shortcomings, he made himself ridiculous. He might never have gone to Hollywood and been the better for it. He might have refused that final squabble over salary that was such a poor imitation of the Babe's perennial battles.

Because these stunts were not done with the usual

fanfare, the fans did not think much of them at the time. Now, however, in the perspective of time, they seem to be the efforts of a man who wanted financial security, an escape from the poverty of his youth — but who, under no circumstances, would trade in his influence with the youngsters who knew him.

If Lou had his own say about his obituary, it would probably not be a poem by Kieran or a eulogy by a city mayor. He probably would have rather had a bunch of kids playing over an unmarked grave somewhere in Central Park where he used to run up and down, shagging flies in his shirtsleeves.

During his playing days Lou never meant as much to the children of the United States as Babe Ruth. But now that the hurlyburly of news print is past, his fame — especially in that onrushing generation that will give baseball its phoenix-like life from year to year — is secure.

It's as Lou said to the Babe once when he got a thundering cheer from a special section of Yankee Stadium where some seven hundred children were seated.

'Gee, Babe,' he said. 'The kids like me.'

THE END

BASEBALL RECORDS

Consecutive games played, 2130
Consecutive years played 150 or more games (tied), 12
Years leading games played, season, 8
Games played season by first baseman (A. L. tied), 157
Games as first baseman (A. L.), 2143
Years leading league in games played by first basemen, 7
Years playing 150 or more games, 12
Runs, game (A. L. tied), 5
Years 100 or more runs, 13
Times five runs in one game, season (tied), 2
Times five runs in one game, league (modern), 3
Consecutive years 100 or more runs, 13
Years 150 or more runs batted in, 7
Consecutive years 150 or more runs batted in (tied), 3
Years 100 or more runs batted in (tied), 13
Consecutive years 100 or more runs batted in, 13
Years leading league in runs batted in (tied), 5
Runs batted in, season (A. L.), 184
Consecutive years 100 or more bases on balls (tied), 5
Times four long hits, game, 5
Long hits, inning (modern, tied), 2
Extra bases, long hits, game (tied), 12
Years 100 or more extra bases on long hits (tied), 14
Consecutive years 100 or more extra bases on long hits, 14
Total bases, game (A. L. tied), 16
Years 400 or more total bases, 5
Consecutive years 400 or more total bases, 2
Years 300 or more total bases, 13
Consecutive years, 300 or more total bases, 13
Home runs, six consecutive games (A. L. tied), 6
Home runs consecutive times at bat (tied), 4
Home runs with bases filled, 23
Home runs with bases filled, season (tied), 4

Home runs, game (tied), 4

Times three or more home runs, game, 4

Home runs, season, against one club on road (tied), 9

Double plays participated in by first baseman, season, 157

Unassisted double plays, first baseman, game (tied), 2

Least chances offered, first baseman two consecutive games (tied), 8

Times only one chance offered, first baseman, game, 2

Times only two or less chances offered, first baseman game, 5

Least chances offered first baseman, season, 150 or more games, 1354

Least put-outs, first baseman, season, 150 or more games, 1284

Least assists first baseman, season, 150 or more games, 58

Least double plays, first baseman, season, 150 or more games, 87

THE COMPLETE BASEBALL RECORD OF LOU GEHRIG

Year	Club	League	Pos.	G.	AB.	R.	H.	2B.	3B.	HR.	RBI.	B.A.	PO.	A.	E.	F.A.
1921 — Hartford	Eastern	1B	12								—	.261	128	4	2	.985
1922 —		Not in organized Ball														
1923 — New York	American	1B	13	26	6	11	4	1	1	9	.423	53	3	6	.903
1923 — Hartford	Eastern	1B	59	227	54	69	13	8	24	—	.304	623	23	6	.991
1924 — New York	American	Util	10	12	2	6	1	0	0	6	.500	10	1	0	1.000
1924 — Hartford	Eastern	1B	134	504	111	186	40	13	37	—	.369	1391	66	23	.984
1925 — New York	American	1B	126	437	73	129	23	10	21	68	.295	1126	53	13	.989
1926 — New York	American	1B	155	572	135	179	47	20	16	107	.313	1566	73	15	.991
1927 — New York	American	1B	155	584	149	218	52	18	47	175	.373	1662	88	15	.991
1928 — New York	American	1B	154	562	139	210	47	13	27	142	.374	1488	79	18	.989
1929 — New York	American	1B	154	553	127	166	33	10	35	126	.300	1458	82	9	.994
1930 — New York	American	1B	154	581	143	220	42	17	41	174	.379	1298	89	15	.989
1931 — New York	American	1B	155	619	163	211	31	15	46	184	.341	1352	58	13	.991
1932 — New York	American	1B	156	596	138	208	42	9	34	151	.349	1293	75	16	.987
1933 — New York	American	1B	152	593	138	198	41	12	32	139	.334	1290	64	9	.993
1934 — New York	American	1B	154	579	128	210	40	6	49	165	.363	1284	80	8	.994
1935 — New York	American	1B	149	535	125	176	26	10	30	119	.329	1377	82	16	.989
1936 — New York	American	1B	155	579	167	205	37	7	49	152	.354	1370	74	9	.994
1937 — New York	American	1B	157	569	138	200	37	9	37	159	.351	1483	100	16	.990
1938 — New York	American	1B	157	576	115	170	32	6	29	114	.295	1337	82	14	.989
1939 — New York	American	1B	8	28	2	4	0	0	0	1	.143	64	4	2	.971
Major League Totals			2164	8001	1888	2721	535	161	494	1991	.340	19511	1087	194	.991

Played under name of Lewis with Hartford in 1921.

WORLD'S SERIES RECORD

Year	Club	League	Pos.	G.	AB.	R.	H.	2B.	3B.	HR.	RBI.	B.A.	PO.	A.	E.	F.A.
1926 — New York	American	1B	7	23	1	8	2	0	0	3	.348	78	1	0	1.000
1927 — New York	American	1B	4	13	2	4	2	2	0	5	.308	41	3	0	1.000
1928 — New York	American	1B	4	11	5	6	1	0	4	9	.545	33	0	0	1.000
1932 — New York	American	1B	4	17	9	9	1	0	3	8	.529	37	2	1	.975
1936 — New York	American	1B	6	24	5	7	1	0	2	7	.292	45	2	0	1.000
1937 — New York	American	1B	5	17	4	5	1	1	1	3	.294	50	1	0	1.000
1938 — New York	American	1B	4	14	4	4	0	0	0	0	.286	25	3	0	1.000
World's Series Totals			34	119	30	43	8	3	10	35	.361	309	12	1	.997

ALL-STAR GAME RECORD

Year	League	Pos.	AB.	R.	H.	2B.	3B.	HR.	RBI.	B.A.	PO.	A.	E.	F.A.
1933 — American		1B	2	0	0	0	0	0	0	.000	12	1	1	.923
1934 — American		1B	4	1	0	0	0	0	0	.000	11	1	1	.923
1935 — American		1B	3	1	0	0	0	0	0	.000	11	0	0	1.000
1936 — American		1B	2	1	1	1	0	1	1	.500	7	1	0	1.000
1937 — American		1B	4	1	2	0	0	1	4	.500	10	0	0	1.000
1938 — American		1B	3	0	1	0	0	0	0	.333	1	0	0	1.000
All-Star Game Totals			18	4	4	1	0	2	5	.222	53	2	2	.964